Masters of cinema

Martin Scorsese

Thomas Sotinel

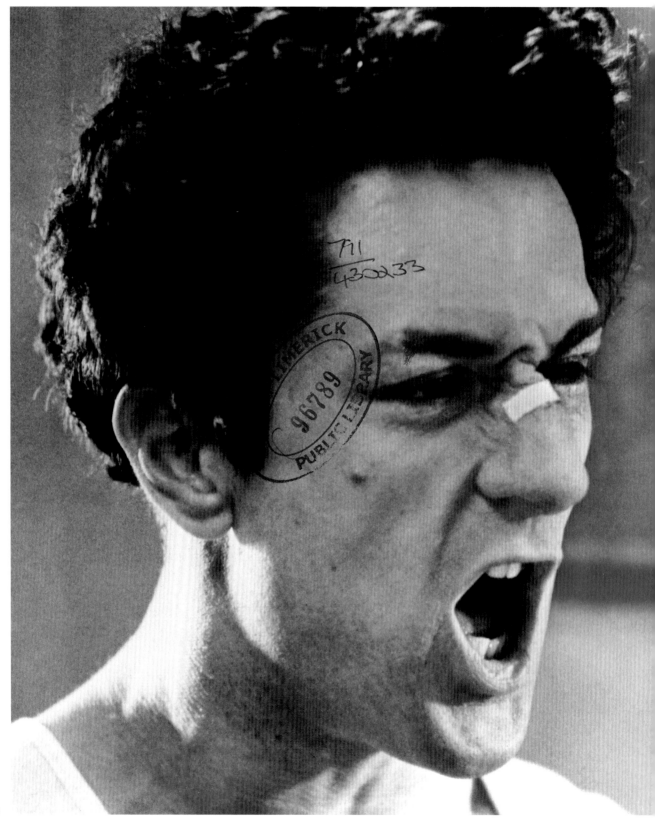

2

Contents

Robert De Niro in *Raging Bull* (1980).

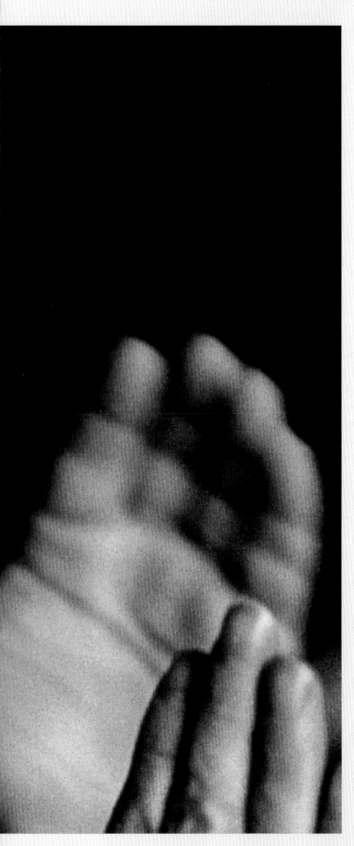

Introduction

In the dim light of a Manhattan church, the little Italian crook praying in front of a *pietà* passes his hand through a candle flame. More than thirty-five years on, that shot from *Mean Streets* remains indelibly imprinted on the visual memory of anyone who saw it at the time. Since then, the director's career has taken many turns yet it already contains the elements that make Martin Scorsese unique in modern cinema: a keen awareness of his origins, a deep knowledge and love of cinema, and an existential anxiety, embodied in characters who inspire terror as well as compassion.

The passing years and their tribulations have enriched Scorsese's subject matter and refined his style, without him ever being untrue to himself. The new decade finds him at the top of his game with two major hits in a row: *The Departed* and *Shutter Island*. However, he has experienced the downs as well as the ups of the American movie industry. The road to the Oscar for Best Picture (for *The Departed*, in 2008) has taken him from the success of *Taxi Driver* in the 1970s to his present exalted status via commercial failures such as *Casino* in 1995.

Scorsese shares disappointments of that kind with other directors of his generation — Francis Ford Coppola, Brian De Palma, Woody Allen … However, unlike them, he has succeeded in avoiding artistic compromise or marginalization, tracing a path in which each one of his films, whether fiction or documentary, personal project or commissioned work, is first and foremost a Martin Scorsese film. This consistency and independence spring from his inexhaustible energy and his formidable diplomatic skills. These qualities have also enabled him to serve cinema as a fierce fighter for the preservation of the cinematic heritage accumulated over the past century.

This brings us to a very American paradox: by building his work on the deceptions and illusions of the dream cherished by all immigrants, Scorsese has forged his own destiny. He has never forgotten that he could have ended up as that petty crook praying at the feet of the Virgin Mary.

Martin Scorsese on the set of *Bringing Out the Dead* (1999).

Background
From Little Italy to the early films

Martin Scorsese during the shooting of *Boxcar Bertha* (1972).

Right: Martin Scorsese and his parents in the late 1940s.

Following pages: Martin, Charles and Catherine Scorsese in *Italianamerican* (1974).

In 1942, Charles and Catherine Scorsese had taken another step towards the American dream. They were living in the New York borough of Queens, on Long Island, a leafy suburb far from the teeming city streets of Little Italy. It was in Queens that Martin was born, on 17 November. The family lived there until 1950, when money troubles forced Charles Scorsese to give up his house and garden, and bring his wife and his two sons, Martin and Frank (six years older), back to Manhattan, to a small apartment on Elizabeth Street, the very street where the parents had grown up in the early years of the twentieth century.

Martin Scorsese has described that return to square one as both a trauma and a privilege. He spent his childhood and adolescence in a ghetto, which made him a quasi-immigrant. That identity gave him the feeling that he was a foreigner in his own country as well as a passionate, painful attachment to it. He would draw on this experience for both his almost enraptured discovery of New York's high society in *The Age of Innocence* (1993) and his agonized portrayal of modern-day corruption in *The Departed* (2006).

As one walks through that part of lower Manhattan today, among its fancy galleries and boutiques, it is almost impossible to imagine what Little Italy was like then. To get an idea of the world in which Martin Scorsese grew up, you have to watch *Mean Streets* (1973), for a first or second time, a film that shows the Italian ghetto just before it was transformed into a smart neighbourhood. The short film *It's Not Just You, Murray!* (1964) paints a more fugitive but even more intimate view of the world that Scorsese knew.

In the mid-twentieth century, Little Italy was a friendly neighbourhood, ideal for raising children. Life was lived according to a calendar imported from the Old World, and the local geography consisted of Catholic churches and shops selling Italian goods, yet the neighbourhood had a double life. There were many respectable shopkeepers and priests, but they counted for little in comparison with the mysterious figures of apparently unemployed men who hung about the streets and inspired a respect mixed with fear.

That was where Charles and Catherine had been born, he in 1912, she in 1913, soon after their parents arrived in New York in 1910. Charles's family was from Pulizzi Generosa, Catherine's from Ciminna, two villages near Palermo, Sicily, and therefore they lived on Elizabeth Street, which was a Sicilian street, but on opposite sides of it. Immigrants

occupied Little Italy's streets and tenement build-
ings according to their geographical roots: Charles
Scorsese's building was lived in by people from
Pulizzi, Catherine Cappa's by those from Ciminna.
When he grew up, Charles Scorsese worked in the
garment industry. As a boy, he supplemented his
income by lighting the stoves and lamps on Saturdays
for families of practising Jews, who also lived in the
neighbourhood. Catherine worked at home as a dress-
maker; she was an expert cook and a model wife.

As their son would remark later, in Sicily a
marriage between Pulizzesi and Ciminnesi would
have been unthinkable. In New York, it was possi-
ble, and their wedding was held in St Patrick's Old
Cathedral, on Mulberry Street. Young Martin found
it strange that the main church in an Italian ghetto
should be dedicated to an Irish saint, until he realized that the immigrants who came from Sicily or
Calabria had won control of the streets of lower
Manhattan in violent battles with the Irish, just as
the Irish had won their place there fifty years earlier. Scorsese was to turn that epic story into his
film *Gangs of New York* (2002).

The little boy experienced his neighbourhood at one remove, however. He suffered from
severe asthma attacks, and had to stay at home and
observe life on the street through his third-floor
bedroom window. It was not until after he had grad-
uated from high school that he discovered the world
beyond the confines of Little Italy. In the meantime,
he studied the microcosm from which his illness
excluded him, while at the same time measuring
it by the yardstick of his only window on the outside world: the cinema.

In the ongoing autobiography that Scorsese
has constructed in interviews and documentaries,
his initiation into cinema plays a central role. He
grew up in a family where books had not found a
place. On the other hand, at the age of four, he saw
King Vidor's *Duel in the Sun* (1946), a melodramatic,
erotic Western starring Jennifer Jones and Gregory
Peck. Of this mega-production, with which its producer David O. Selznick hoped to repeat the success
of *Gone with the Wind* (1939), the little boy retained
a vivid, violent memory that he describes in the
opening of his documentary anthology, *A Personal
Journey with Martin Scorsese Through American Movies*
(1995). He relates how he was always covering his
eyes with his hands, and how everything seemed

to suggest that the two protagonists could express their passion only by killing one another.

As Martin's asthma became worse, his father took him to the cinema more and more often. He was blessed with a prodigious memory, and began to lay down the rudiments of what would become one of the century's most impressive funds of knowledge about cinema. Then TV made its entrance into the Scorsese home, complementing this education. It enabled Martin to discover a different cinema from that of the Manhattan movie theatres: Italian neo-realist films, British films by Michael Powell and Emeric Pressburger, who made *Black Narcissus* (1947) and *The Red Shoes* (1948); films whose narrative imagination and extravagant colours were a departure from the Hollywood norm.

The great events in the world of cinema that punctuated Martin Scorsese's childhood in fact marked the death throes of the old Hollywood, from the magnificent artistic and financial failure of *Duel in the Sun* (1946) to the premiere of Henry Koster's *The Robe* (1953). This melodrama set in the early days of Christianity was the first film to be made in Cinemascope, a wide-screen format created in the hope of countering the advance of TV.

During this time, Martin Scorsese went from one Catholic school to another. When he was eleven years old, a priest of an unusual kind, young and open-minded, made a strong impression on him. Martin attended Mass every Sunday and as he was approaching his teens, he began to think about training for the priesthood. But just before his fourteenth birthday, Elvis Presley burst upon American TV screens. Scorsese has said that it was rock and roll that diverted him from his vocation. In any case, by 1956, he was hanging out in the streets of

Opposite page: Joe Morale, a friend of Martin Scorsese, photographed in Little Italy by Scorsese himself, in the early 1960s.

Above: Peter Bermuth in *The Big Shave* (1967).

Below: Martin Scorsese on the set of *What's a Nice Girl Like You Doing in a Place Like This?* (1963).

his neighbourhood with youths whose lives later turned out badly. He just managed to graduate from high school, and at the start of the 1960s, found himself at Washington Square College, part of New York University (NYU).

Scorsese the student

To reach Washington Square from Elizabeth Street, you only have to cross Houston Street, thus entering Greenwich Village, something Scorsese swears he had never done before. His immersion in the university world brought a host of new experiences. He discovered that not all girls were brunettes and that you could talk about films for hours on end.

At NYU, the cinema courses were taught by Haig Manoogian, an Armenian-American intellectual, born in 1916, who did all he could to discourage dilettantes. He had no great regard for the Hollywood 'product', and instead opened his students' eyes to the great directors of the silent age, to experimental cinema and to European *auteurs*. With his exacting standards, he soon realized that Scorsese took cinema seriously.

At the university itself and in New York's cinephile circles, Scorsese soon found kindred spirits. There were his contemporaries: Michael Wadleigh, the future director of *Woodstock* (1970); Mardik Martin, who worked with Scorsese on several

screenplays up to and including *Raging Bull* (1980); and Brian De Palma, who was the first of them to emigrate to Hollywood after making his early films in New York with a young actor called Robert De Niro. And there were his seniors: John Cassavetes, who had just begun his career as an independent director with *Shadows*, released in 1959, which showed precisely how one could film on the streets of New York, bringing to life characters taken from real life; and Jonas Mekas, the avant-garde director who wrote the film column in the *Village Voice*, the weekly paper of the burgeoning counter-culture.

First steps

In 1963, under Manoogian's tutelage, Scorsese made *What's a Nice Girl Like You Doing in a Place Like This?*, his first student film. Lasting nine minutes, it is an absurd tale that shows the journey to adulthood of a writer who is fascinated by a painting of no inherent interest, a chromolithograph of a man in a boat on a lake.

It's Not Just You, Murray! (1964).

Opposite page: Sam De Fazio in *It's Not Just You, Murray!* (1964).

12

Adolescent and irritating as the film is, it was sufficiently competent to win a prize of $1,000, awarded in June 1964 by the Society of Cinematologists.

Manoogian considers Scorsese one of the best students he has ever had, an opinion confirmed by *It's Not Just You, Murray!*, made in 1964. This portrait of a thug, based on one of his uncles, is marked by a certain casualness, and a spirit of mockery that would later disappear entirely from Scorsese's films. But one can also see emerging a talent for directing actors, a mastery of pace and a concern with the truthfulness of his characters that would become the hallmarks of his work. The young director presents a man in his fifties glorying in the material rewards he has obtained in thirty years of criminal activity, from Prohibition to the 1960s. The film is studded with references to other films: using half a dozen dancers, Scorsese sketches a musical scene in the style of Busby Berkeley's elaborate geometrical numbers in 1930s musicals, and the end of the film evokes Fellini at the risk of falling into pastiche, pure and simple.

Scorsese received his BA, majoring in English, and went on to obtain an MA at NYU. In 1967, he made *The Big Shave*, a short film that shows a man shaving in front of his mirror to the point of self-mutilation. Scorsese told Michael Henry Wilson[1] that he had planned to end this bloody episode with shots of the war in Vietnam, before deciding that the film was explicit enough.

Manoogian now had absolute confidence in him and did not intervene in any way in the making of his graduation film. Scorsese somehow managed to shoot it in 35mm, something unprecedented in the history of the NYU film school. *Bring on the Dancing Girls* was already a feature film seventy minutes long when it was shown for the first time in November 1965, but it would be another four years before it acquired its final form, which was as *Who's That Knocking at My Door?*

In 1965 it had already cost $7,000, when the budget for graduation films was usually no more than $400. The money came from the university and the Scorsese family. Catherine Scorsese had been brought in to help, both as an actress and to work in the canteen, while Charles had dipped into his savings.

The film was screened in the auditorium of NYU's law department. In his interviews with Wilson, Scorsese recalls it as a 'disaster' but the review published in the *New York Times*[2] was full of praise, highlighting the young director's 'raw vitality' and 'fertile imagination'. There was no thought at that stage of commercial distribution.

Martin Scorsese now had his degree. He married Laraine Marie Brennan, at St Patrick's Old Cathedral, although he had lost his faith. Their daughter Catherine was born in 1965. The immediate question was his professional future: as he told the *Times*, in the article on *Bring on the Dancing Girls*, he was not very optimistic about being able to pursue personal projects. He took as his role model Orson Welles, who made his first feature film when he was only thirty, and he had just seen Bernardo Bertolucci's *Before the Revolution* (1964), at the second New York Film Festival, in 1964. The young Italian director, who would go on to make *Last Tango in Paris* (1972), was only twenty-two, like Scorsese himself, a fact he found encouraging.

Haig Manoogian was convinced that *Bring on the Dancing Girls* could be a 'real' film. He persuaded Scorsese to go back to it and shoot new scenes with Harvey Keitel,(who had to give up work as a court stenographer for this). Keitel was three years older than Scorsese, and had started out working in the theatre. Scorsese found in this young Jew from Brooklyn the perfect interpreter of the alter egos that he put at the centre of his first screenplays. Here he plays J. R., a young man who spends his days hanging round the streets of Little Italy with his friends. The film, entitled *Who's That Knocking at My Door?*, is the second part of a trilogy. The first part, *Jerusalem, Jerusalem* — which was never made — is the story of a religious retreat attended by a group of teenagers obsessed with sex and racked by feelings of guilt. The third, *Season of the Witch*, shows its hero falling into the alternative world of organized crime.

Below, top: Kirk Douglas and Lana Turner in Vincente Minnelli's *The Bad and the Beautiful* (1952).

Below, bottom: Judy Garland and Mickey Rooney in Busby Berkeley's *Babes in Arms* (1939).

Scorsese: cineaste and cinephile

From the start, Martin Scorsese took his place in cinema history, making his influences. Over the years, his love of cinema has taken the form of a constant concern to preserve and transmit this inheritance. In 1979, he launched an appeal to alert his colleagues and the general public to the dangers to which American films shot in colour since the 1950s were exposed. The Eastman process, which had replaced Technicolor, quickly degrades, both as negatives and as projection copies. Scorsese conducted a successful campaign for the preservation of these films and establish such good relations with Eastman-Kodak that since 1992 his film collection has been held at the George Eastman House, the museum dedicated to Kodak's founder,

in Rochester, New York. For Scorsese is also a collector. At first he accumulated thousands of video cassettes, employing an assistant to record and classify this collection, which was suddenly enlarged by the appearance of cable TV. In 1988, in *The Scorsese Machine*, a film in the series 'Cinéma, de notre temps' made by André S. Labarthe, we see the exhilarating effect on Scorsese of the arrival of the Turner Classic Movies (TCM) channel in New York TV schedules. At the same time, he scrupulously preserves the archives of each of his projects; amounting to several hundred volumes, these are currently being digitized at the Milan Cinematheque. In 1990, with the support of many of his colleagues, including Woody Allen, Robert Altman, Francis Ford Coppola and Clint

Eastwood, Scorsese set up the Film Foundation, whose purpose is to raise funds to restore great film classics. Films restored to their original splendour under this programme include John Ford's *How Green Was My Valley* (1941), Charles Laughton's *The Night of the Hunter* (1955) and Alfred Hitchcock's *Shadow of a Doubt* (1943).

Shortly afterwards, Scorsese embarked on two films devoted to his vision of cinema history. In *A Personal Journey with Martin Scorsese Through American Movies* (1995), which he made with Michael Henry Wilson, he lists the films that helped him develop his aesthetic – from Vincente Minnelli's *The Bad and the Beautiful* (1952) to little-known films noirs such as Abraham Polonsky's *Force of Evil* (1948) – and at the same time

sketches a history of the social and artistic status of filmmakers in the United States. In his typology of directors, it is not difficult to recognize Scorsese's various avatars: an 'iconoclast', like Welles, at the beginning, then a 'pirate', like Tourneur, when necessity required it.

My Voyage to Italy (*Il Mio Viaggio in Italia*, 2001) is more like an anthology – the excerpts from films are much longer – and it has a much narrower time-frame, since it is devoted essentially to neo-realism and its early mutations, up to the great films made by Antonioni, Visconti and Fellini in the early 1960s. The two films taken together give a fair idea of the geography of Scorsese's cinematic world, if we add to it a number of other heroes such as Michael Powell and Jean Renoir.

Who's That Knocking at My Door?

Who's That Knocking at My Door? progressed slowly. Scorsese found an actress, Zina Bethune, and shot new scenes in 16mm with her and Keitel, which he had to match with the first version's 35mm sequences. Finally, in November 1967, four years after its screening at NYU, the film was shown at the Chicago Film Festival. Roger Ebert, the critic of the *Chicago Sun Times*, who was then one of the advocates of young American cinema, wrote an article in its praise that was almost ecstatic. But it still had not found a distributor. Until, that is, Joseph Brenner, a specialist in pornographic films who wanted to gain a little respectability, made an offer to Manoogian: he would take the film on if Scorsese would agree to add some nude scenes. Scorsese was in Europe at the time. He sent for Keitel, who joined him in the Netherlands, and hired a French actress, Anne Colette, who had appeared in Godard's *All the Boys Are Called Patrick* (1957). The film finally came out in New York in 1969. Reviews were favourable on the whole. John Cassavetes expressed his approval, but the public didn't flock to the film.

Who's That Knocking at My Door? shows the marks of its long gestation, but also possesses some of the dominant features of Scorsese's films: the verbal intensity, the confident handling of the cinematography and the use of popular music that becomes the soundtrack for a piece of fiction after providing the background to everyday life. And the director's obsessions — violence and guilt — make their thunderous entrance: Scorsese shows a disastrous love scene, shot in his parents' bed.

But he was still unsure which direction he should take. In 1968, he messed up his Hollywood debut by getting himself fired at the end of the first week from the set of *The Honeymoon Killers*, a black comedy eventually made by Leonard Kastle in 1970. Scorsese admits that his dismissal was justified: after seven days he had shot only a few pages of the screenplay.

Scorsese now got a divorce, obtained his PhD at NYU, worked on the editing of *Woodstock* (1970), directed by his friend Michael Wadleigh, taught at the university and made a few unfortunate forays into advertising. In 1970, he coordinated a politically

Opposite page: on the set of *Who's That Knocking at My Door?* (1969). From top to bottom: Martin Scorsese with Harvey Keitel and Mardik Martin; Harvey Keitel and Zina Bethune; Max Fisher (centre) and Anne Colette.

Right: Harvey Keitel and Martin Scorsese on the set of *Street Scenes* (1970).

militant film, *Street Scenes*, shot during demonstrations against the war in Vietnam. He only directed the scene of the final debate, in which he took part. The anti-war movement was falling apart at the time, and the experience left a bitter taste in his mouth.

Early in 1971, he left for Hollywood again, at the invitation of the producer of *Woodstock*, Freddie Weintraub, who worked for Warner Bros.

Boxcar Bertha

Although Scorsese was suffering frequent asthma attacks and felt increasingly unwell on the West Coast, the producer and director Roger Corman suggested that he direct *Boxcar Bertha* (1972). Corman, who had set up his own studio, American Independent Pictures (AIP), was the king of violent, low-budget horror films. He had given work to many promising newcomers, including Jack Nicholson, Peter Fonda and Francis Ford Coppola.

AIP was a small studio, then in its glory days. To the previous decade's horror films, including the famous adaptations from Edgar Allen Poe made by Corman himself, it had added productions that rode the counter-cultural wave: stories about bikers, drugs and anarchistic criminals. Based on the dubiously authentic autobiography of a female union activist who became a bank robber in the Great Depression, *Boxcar Bertha* is a direct descendant of Arthur Penn's *Bonnie and Clyde*, whose success in 1967 marked the beginning of what would be dubbed the 'New Hollywood', the period when for a short time directors were the power-brokers in the film industry.

Its stars were Barbara Hershey and David Carradine, and Scorsese has described how Corman gave him the script, saying: 'Read the script, rewrite as much as you want, but remember, Marty, that you must have some nudity every fifteen pages.'[3] In the end, Scorsese didn't rewrite all that much. Of course, he gave two minor characters the names Michael Powell and Emeric Pressburger, and made the character of the Yankee poker-player, played by Barry Primus, into a kind of alter ego, an energetic, hyper-anxious New Yorker who is lost and far from home. But he stuck to the essence of the story: a doomed romance between an independent, uninhibited, very young girl and an anarchist union leader, who ends up being crucified on the door of a goods wagon. When people have seen this Christlike ending as prefiguring films to come, beginning with *The Last Temptation of Christ* (1988), Scorsese has always replied that the scene was already there in Joyce Hooper Carrington's screenplay, and that it had seemed to him like a 'gift from heaven'.

The shoot, in California and Arkansas, where the action of the film takes place, went well. Scorsese kept to the budget of $700,000 he had been given. Anxious not to repeat the fiasco of *The Honeymoon Killers*, he drew out every shot anticipated in the shooting script, a technique he would often use again. Roger Corman was happy with the result. When the film was released, in August 1972, some critics, such as Roger Ebert and Howard Thompson, in the *New York Times*, said *Boxcar Bertha* was not 17 a simple exploitation movie. But when Scorsese showed it to John Cassavetes, he said, 'Nice work, but don't fucking ever do something like this again'. 'Why don't you make a movie about something you really care about?'[4]

Boxcar Bertha does not entirely deserve that negative response from the man who made *Faces* (1968). The film was effective, and Barbara Hershey was naked; Scorsese had kept to his agreement with Corman, as he would generally keep his commitments to his producers, Disney in the case of *The Color of Money* (1986) and Spielberg for *Cape Fear* (1991). But he had also succeeded in directing the mandatory massacre scenes in a different way, which clearly defines the arbitrary nature of violence and rejects stylized choreography, and he managed to give the character of Bertha a dignity and stature that would later be shared by Alice in *Alice Doesn't Live Here Anymore* (1974) and Ellen Olenska in *The Age of Innocence* (1993).

All in all, the outcome was positive: Scorsese had proved that he could make a film under real professional conditions, and he had not shaken the critical credit he had won with *Who's That Knocking at My Door?* He prepared to follow Cassavetes's advice and shoot the third part of his trilogy. His friend Jay Cocks, *Time* magazine's film critic, had come up with a new title for *Season of the Witch*, a phrase borrowed from Raymond Chandler's *The Simple Art of Murder* – *Mean Streets*.

Warren Beatty and Faye Dunaway in Arthur Penn's *Bonnie and Clyde* (1967).

Opposite page: Barbara Hershey and David Carradine in *Boxcar Bertha* (1972).

Mean Streets

From *Mean Streets* to *The King of Comedy*

Harvey Keitel in *Mean Streets* (1973).

Following pages: David Proval and
Robert De Niro in *Mean Streets* (1973).

Roger Corman was delighted with *Boxcar Bertha*, and offered to produce *Mean Streets* for Scorsese on one condition: he wanted to move the action from Little Italy to Harlem and to cast African-American actors, hoping in this way to repeat the success of *Shaft* (1971). Scorsese thought about it, and decided to shoot the film as he intended, even though he had a tiny budget of $500,000, raised by a young producer from the rock scene, Jonathan Taplin. For the casting, Scorsese returned to Harvey Keitel, who again played the director's alter ego, this time, called Charlie. An actor to play his friend and nemesis, Johnny Boy, still had to be found.

Robert De Niro also grew up in Little Italy, a few blocks from Elizabeth Street. Scorsese had run into him a few times, but did not really get to know him until late 1970, when they were introduced by Brian De Palma, who had used De Niro in his early films. The young actor had just made his Hollywood debut in a melodrama about sport, *Bang the Drum Slowly* (1973), and at first he wanted to play Charlie. But Scorsese wouldn't drop Harvey Keitel and so De Niro had to be content with the shorter role of Johnny Boy.

In the spring of 1973, his budget did not allow Scorsese to shoot everything in New York, as he would have liked. The interiors were shot in Los Angeles, and the crew had only a week to do the exteriors in the streets of Little Italy. The residents took umbrage at the title, *Mean Streets*, written in chalk on the clapperboard. Charles Scorsese told his son that he could have avoided misunderstandings if he had allowed him to prepare the ground.

The crew then left for Los Angeles. Scorsese did not have much time, but devoted what little he had to his actors, allowing them great freedom. The most brilliant effects of this approach are found at the beginning of the film, in a long, almost entirely improvised, exchange between Keitel and De Niro. The dialogue is not brilliant, and is repetitive, but it comes over as accurate and violent, giving these petty thugs who are scarcely more than teenagers an immediate humanity that sets them apart from the usual stereotypes of film noir. When Scorsese showed his family and friends a first cut of *Mean Streets*, Cassavetes found things to admire in this sequence, while De Palma advised him to cut it.

Mean Streets was both the culmination of Scorsese's years of training, and his first major film. For the last time, he used directly autobiographical material and a screenplay, which, even if it passed through several hands (including those of Mardik

Martin and Jay Cocks), primarily reflected his own experience. The sequences that show Charlie praying and the relationships among young men hovering on the brink of a life of crime all go back to the stories Scorsese made from the material of his childhood and youth. He stamped this personal material with the mark of a great director, with confidence in his craft, able to create fluid long shots to capture a chaotic fight in a billiard hall. It's a way of giving shape to movement that doesn't simply accompany the narration but accelerates it. *Mean Streets* contains so many features that have become commonplace in popular cinema — the use of slow motion at unexpected moments, music, and dialogue made up of three words shouted back and forth — that it is hard to imagine today the impact they had at the time. This new grammar of violence is combined with an existential unease that has no equivalent among Scorsese's contemporaries, who were more interested in social commentary. The final distinctive feature is that *Mean Streets*, a film anchored in contemporary reality, is also imbued with cinema history in all its forms of expression. We glimpse snatches of *The Tomb of Ligeia* (1965), one of Roger Corman's adaptations of Poe; of John Ford's *The Searchers* (1956); and Fritz Lang's *The Big Heat* (1953).

     Mean Streets was completed in summer 1973, and was greeted with great enthusiasm at the New York Film Festival. The following year, it was selected for the Directors' Fortnight at Cannes. To Scorsese's great delight, Warner Bros. agreed to distribute it, and it was released in the United States in October 1973, when it joined the ranks of the great films noirs. Pauline Kael, film critic of the *New Yorker* and the 'muse' of the New Hollywood since she defended *Bonnie and Clyde* against the establishment in the shape of Bosley Crowther (long-time film critic for the *New York Times*), sang its praises, seeing in *Mean Streets* the 'best film American of the year'.

Alice Doesn't Live Here Anymore

It was Warner Bros., headed by John Calley, that offered the young prodigy his first chance to work for a major studio. Basking in the glow of her success in William Friedkin's *The Exorcist* (1973), the actress Ellen Burstyn was able to choose her next screenplay, and she went for *Alice Doesn't Live Here Anymore*, an original script by Robert Getchell, about

John Wayne in John Ford's *The Searchers* (1956).

Opposite page: Martin Scorsese on the set of *Mean Streets* (1973).

24

a young widow who flees New Mexico with her little boy, hoping to resume her career as a singer which had been interrupted by her marriage. Francis Ford Coppola was the 'big brother' of this generation, who were in the process of establishing themselves in Hollywood. He had dipped into his wallet to support the production of *Mean Streets* and had chosen De Niro to play the young Vito Corleone in *The Godfather Part II* (1974). He was successful in suggesting Scorsese's name to Calley and Burstyn.

The young man survived quite well his first experience of working with a major studio. He was able to make the screenplay 'tougher' by introducing an element of ambiguity into the original happy ending, and was allowed to improvise several sequences. He devoted a good part of a comfortable budget — three times that of *Mean Streets* — to building a set used only in the opening sequence. It shows Alice as a child on a farm in the Midwest,

Mia Bendixsen in *Alice Doesn't Live Here Anymore* (1974).

Opposite page: Kris Kristofferson and Ellen Burstyn in *Alice Doesn't Live Here Anymore* (1974).

Right: Judy Garland in Victor Fleming's *The Wizard of Oz* (1939).

and is reminiscent of the artificial colours of melodramas like Douglas Sirk's *Imitation of Life* (1959), or *Gone with the Wind* and *The Wizard of Oz* (1939).

Once this whimsical passage is over, the film takes a route more conventional for the time. Scorsese introduces moments of tension — like the episode of the affair between Alice and Ben, an ultra-violent fantasist whom Harvey Keitel makes terrifying — but the film to a large extent preserves the screenplay's optimism. Scorsese had estimated a running length of three and a half hours, but he was forced to make a version lasting less than two. It opened in a Los Angeles cinema in December 1974, so that it could compete in the Oscars. And Ellen Burstyn did in fact win the award for best leading actress. Since *Alice Doesn't Live Here Anymore* took a great deal of money — over $15 million — and was presented in competition at Cannes in 1975, Martin Scorsese could pride himself on being a member of the Hollywood élite.

Taxi Driver

No sooner was he back from Cannes than Scorsese immediately began to draw on that fund of capital. During the summer of 1975, on the humid New York streets, the former student of the Jesuits began directing a screenplay written by the most puritanical figure of New Hollywood, Paul Schrader. He had just joined the studio system, and sold the screenplay of *Yakuza* (1974), to be directed by Sidney Pollack, for a very large sum. The script of *Taxi Driver* (1976) was originally intended for Robert Mulligan

and Jeff Bridges, but it was bought by the producers Michael and Julia Phillips, who offered it to Scorsese with the screenwriter's approval. The streets are still every bit as mean, and Robert De Niro's name is in the credits again, this time heading the cast.

But *Taxi Driver* is a fundamentally different film from *Mean Streets*. The community has disappeared, and the city is no longer a natural environment but the projection of the fantasies and fears of one man. Travis Bickle, a veteran of the Vietnam War that has not long ended, lives inside a broken mind.

Determined to purge the city of its abominations, Travis feels he is charged with a divine mission, like Ethan Edwards, the avenger in John Ford's *The Searchers*, a figure constantly evoked in the films of the young American filmmakers of the day. Cut off from the outside world, Travis sees it only through a succession of hallucinations peopled by repulsive characters: the voyeuristic, homicidal husband, played by Scorsese himself, the pimp played by Harvey Keitel, who puts a teenager on the streets (Jodie Foster, whom Scorsese had already cast brilliantly in *Alice Doesn't Live Here Anymore*).

The precision and power of these visions lie in the shot-by-shot shooting script that Scorsese had drawn up before filming started. It allowed him to keep De Niro's brilliant improvisations within a rigorous frame. Michael Chapman's cinematography, which makes the city's lights shimmer and captures its toxic exhalations, heightens the sense of rising violence, until an apocalyptic finale that Scorsese was obliged to soften a little (toning down the red of the blood that pours out after Travis's slaughter) so that the film could be shown to minors.

These changes did nothing to reduce *Taxi Driver*'s tremendous impact, further enhanced by

Taxi Driver, by Pauline Kael

Scorsese may just naturally be an Expressionist; his asthmatic bedridden childhood in a Sicilian-American home in Little Italy propelled him toward a fix on the violently exciting movies he saw. Physically and intellectually, he's a speed demon, a dervish. Even in *Alice Doesn't Live Here Anymore* he found a rationale for restless, whirlwind movement. But Scorsese is also the most carnal of directors – movement is ecstatic for him – and that side of him didn't come out in *Alice*. This new movie gives him a chance for the full Expressionist use of the city which he was denied in *Mean Streets*, because it was set in New York but was made on a minuscule budget in southern California, with only seven shooting days in New York itself. Scorsese's Expressionism isn't anything like the exaggerated sets of the German directors; he uses documentary locations, but he pushes discordant elements to their limits, and the cinematographer, Michael Chapman, gives the street life a seamy, rich pulpiness. When Travis is taunted by a pimp, Sport (Harvey Keitel), the pimp is so eager for action that he can't stand still; the hipster with his rhythmic jiggling, makes an eerily hostile contrast to the paralyzed, dumbfounded Travis. Scorsese gets the quality of trance in a scene like this; the whole movie has a sense of vertigo. Scorsese's New York is the big city of the thrillers he feasted his imagination on – but at a later stage of decay. This New York is a voluptuous enemy. The street vapors become ghostly; Sport the pimp romancing his baby whore leads her in a hypnotic dance; the porno theatres are like mortuaries; the congested traffic is macabre. And this Hell is always in movement...

Some actors are said to be empty vessels who are filled by the roles they play, but that's not what appears to be happening here with De Niro. He's gone the other way. He's used his emptiness – he's reached down into his own anomie. Only Brando has done this kind of plunging, and De Niro's performance has something of the undistanced intensity that Brando's had in *Last Tango*. In its own way, this movie, too, has an erotic aura. There is practically no sex in it, but no sex can be as disturbing as sex. And that's what it's about: the absence of sex – bottled-up, impacted energy and emotion, with a blood-splattering release. The fact that we experience Travis's need for an explosion viscerally, and that the explosion itself has the quality of consummation, makes *Taxi Driver* one of the few truly modern horror films.

This is an extract from 'Underground Man', published in *The New Yorker*, 9 February 1976.

Opposite page: Martin Scorsese with Cybill Shepherd on the set of *Taxi Driver* (1976).

Right: Martin Scorsese with Harvey Keitel (top) and Robert De Niro (top and bottom) on the set of *Taxi Driver* (1976).

Following pages: Jodie Foster and Robert De Niro in *Taxi Driver* (1976).

The massacre in *Taxi Driver* and the concluding dinner in *The Age of Innocence*

In 1976, with *Taxi Driver*, Martin Scorsese received his confirmation as an international director, in the form of a Palme d'Or at Cannes. Throughout the film, he puts into practice, with an intensity he had not achieved before, the two impulses that come to him when he thinks about directing a situation: first of all, using a method – framing, light, sound – that he has put together in the course of his long exploration of cinema, then correcting and adapting it – often to the point where it is unrecognizable – until it yields to the necessity of expressing the required emotion.

From this point of view, the final massacre sequence is an exemplary illustration. From the moment when Travis Bickle asks the pimp, Sport, if he's carrying a gun, to the shot of Travis pretending to shoot himself in the head, only six minutes pass, which Scorsese manipulates by accelerating the pace – the john, riddled with bullets, who totters backwards and collapses at the feet of the child prostitute – or slowing it down – the injured hotelkeeper pursuing Bickle along the corridor. The length of the shots varies from the long take, showing the first confrontation between Travis and Sport – almost a minute and a half, with a violent climax well before the end of the shot – to the subliminal shots of the corridors and the stairs (places that recur almost obsessively in Scorsese's work), at first, before

the final massacre, simply filthy, then covered in blood. Towards the end of the sequence, a direct high-angle shot, for which the ceiling of the apartment had to be cut away, shows Travis, barely alive, among the bodies.

Seventeen years later, Scorsese brought *The Age of Innocence* to its conclusion with a dinner-table scene as civilized as the massacre in *Taxi Driver* is barbarous. But the main character, Newland Archer, is no longer there. He has said it himself a few shots previously: 'I am dead.' This dinner forces him into the company of the living. The evening puts the seal on his separation from Countess Olenska, under pressure from his family and class, and of course from his wife, May. A first shot skims over the table before coming back to linger over the faces of the guests.

The next shot isolates Archer, stopping on his chest, where his heart beats, where, in a pocket that magically becomes transparent – Scorsese likes to use these unusual effects, which with his very contemporary, fluid way of moving the camera, regain their original impact – we see the key of the bedroom where Archer and the Countess were to have slept, which she has returned to him. Archer's total solitude, in the midst of what the voiced-over narration describes as an 'armed camp' in which he was a 'prisoner', is as terrible as Travis's among the dead bodies.

Above, top: Jodie Foster and Robert De Niro in *Taxi Driver* (1976).

Above, bottom: Richard E. Grant and Michelle Pfeiffer in *The Age of Innocence* (1993).

Opposite page: Robert De Niro in *Taxi Driver* (1976).

the haunting score from the veteran composer Bernard Herrmann, who wrote music for Welles and Hitchcock. Scorsese himself was disconcerted by some reactions to the film. He said, 'I saw *Taxi Driver* once in a theatre, on the opening night, I think, and everyone was yelling and screaming at the shoot-out. When I made it, I didn't intend to have the audience react with that feeling. "Yes, do it! Let's go out and kill!" The idea was to create a violent catharsis, so that they'd find themselves saying, "Yes, kill"; and then afterwards realize, "My God, no" — like some strange Californian therapy session.'[5]

Based on a real person who tried to assassinate Governor George Wallace of Alabama in 1972, Travis Bickle has become the model for would-be murderers, including John Hinckley, who in 1981 fired at President Reagan to show his love for Jodie Foster.

Probably because he expresses so precisely the depressive, hyperactive mood of the day — America's defeat in Vietnam and the warning signs of Reaganite conservatism — *Taxi Driver* enjoyed, against all expectations, great success with audiences. Internationally, the award of the Palme d'Or at Cannes in 1976 meant that Scorsese's reputation was securely established.

Scorsese and music

Confined to his bedroom on Elizabeth Street, the young Martin Scorsese would watch what was going on in the street below, but he didn't even need to go to the window to hear the soundtrack. He has described it as a mixture of everyday sounds and music – popular American songs drifting from radio sets, bel canto arias played on gramophones, and people humming tunes: he told Clara and Robert Kuperberg in their documentary, *Martin Scorsese, l'émotion par la musique* (2005), how the soundtrack of his life had been determined by his environment – it was a cacophony.

In *Scorsese on Scorsese*, he says (p.28): 'I remember one time looking out of the window, a block away from a bar, seeing two bums staggering down Elizabeth Street, one so drunk the other's stealing his shoes, and while this fight was going on I could hear from somewhere "When My Dream Boat Comes Home" by Fats Domino. That was just how crazy this world actually was, and it made me think, why don't they do that in films?' He applied this method from the beginning, using the music of everyday life and rejecting the kind of redundancy that insists on a love song in a love scene, preferring the effect of violent contrasts. In 1969, his first feature film, *Who's That Knocking at My Door?*, took its title from a song by an obscure vocal group from Long Beach, the Genies, which is heard on the soundtrack, a mixture of contemporary rock, Mitch Ryder and the Detroit Wheels, and old numbers from a decade or so earlier, in the doo-wop style. With *Mean Streets*, Scorsese had achieved a sort of perfection: syrupy Phil Spector songs like 'Be My Baby', by the Ronettes, make a powerful contrast with the violence of the relations between the characters; the entrance of Johnnie Boy (Robert De Niro) and Charlie (Harvey Keitel) into the bar is turned into a spectacle by the use of the Rolling Stones' 'Jumpin' Jack Flash'.

This method was not suitable for every film. For *Taxi Driver*, which takes place entirely in the mental space of a single character, the exterior sounds are always distorted. To portray Travis Bickle's isolation, Scorsese turned to Bernard Herrmann, one of 'old' Hollywood's great composers; he wrote the score for Orson Welles's *Citizen Kane*, in 1941, and worked with Alfred Hitchcock. Not only did Scorsese have to put pressure on the old man, who was reluctant to come out of retirement, but he also forced him use a language with which he had hitherto been unfamiliar: jazz. The score was a success, but Herrmann died on the last evening of recording, 24 December 1975. Throughout his career, Scorsese has alternated the two options, using other great Hollywood composers, such as Elmer Bernstein, for *Cape Fear*, and rock musicians like Peter Gabriel, for *The Last Temptation of Christ*, in a search for original soundtracks that have become an inseparable part of these films. And his great criminal epics, *Goodfellas*, *Casino*, and *The Departed*, are accompanied by virtuoso collages. In *Casino*, we hear the Rolling Stones' 'Can't You Hear Me Knocking', as well as Bach's St Matthew Passion. 'Because', as Scorsese puts it in the documentary *Martin Scorsese, l'émotion par la musique*, 'as rotten as they are, these characters are human beings, and they deserve Bach'.

Opposite page: Robert De Niro in *New York, New York* (1977).

Right: Liza Minnelli in *New York, New York* (1977).

New York, New York

New York, New York (1977), Scorsese's next film, is a monument to frustration and disappointment. On the basis of an incomplete screenplay by Earl Mac Rauch, revised by his long-time collaborator Mardik Martin and by Julia Cameron, whom Scorsese had married in December 1975, he hoped to pour the New Cinema material into the old Hollywood mould, and shoot a musical on studio sets, bringing to life characters who would be as intense, complex and real as those of *Mean Streets*.

It was 1976, and Francis Ford Coppola was shooting *Apocalypse Now*. The younger generation wanted to prove they could make films that were as big and as beautiful as those of their revered predecessors — King Vidor, Howard Hawks or, in Scorsese's case, Vincente Minnelli. As it happened, the female lead in *New York, New York* fell to the daughter of Judy Garland and the director of *The Bad and the Beautiful* (1952): Liza Minnelli. She plays Francine Evans, a gifted singer who falls in love with a saxophonist called Jimmy Doyle, an angry, demanding man and a liar, with the physical features of Robert De Niro — the actor learned to play the tenor saxophone for the role — and the character, as he himself admitted, of Martin Scorsese.

The impossible love of an artist dedicated to her career and a musician torn between self-discipline and his thirst for instant gratification was not the ideal theme with which to recreate the enchanted world of the musicals of the 1950s.

Opposite page: Joni Mitchell and
The Band in *The Last Waltz* (1978).

Above: Martin Scorsese on the set
of *New York, New York* (1977).

The shoot was very long. Scorsese wanted
to allow his actors to improvise, but what was
easy in the back-room of a café suddenly became
difficult when it had to be done on a set costing
tens of thousands of dollars, while extras waited
around for days with nothing to do. This was also
the moment when Scorsese, who since early childhood had been living with the support of prescrip-
tion drugs, believed he had found relief in cocaine;
during the shoot of *New York, New York* he began a
journey from which he would emerge only five
years later, barely alive.

Despite these initial problems, *New York, New
York* is a big film, so sensual and full of energy that
one hesitates to call it a failure. Granted, the open-
ing scene, the first meeting between Francine and
Jimmy on the evening of the celebrations of the
United States' victory over Japan in 1945, seems   37

to last for hours. Robert De Niro's clumsy and brutal attempts at seduction are so unpleasant to watch that one wonders how he ever became a star. But this sequence, which any sensible producer would have demanded be cut, is also one of the finest depictions of the war between the sexes ever filmed.

This time Scorsese exercises his virtuosity in the studio, and he combines the style of the old masters with his own fluid camera movements. The result is both frustrating, because he is filming nothing but an accumulation of frustrations, and exhilarating, because this new alliance between the raw humanity of the characters and the artificiality of the images is almost always successful. It remains to be said, however, that the film was a commercial and, in the United States, critical failure.

The Last Waltz

Scorsese did not take the time to draw any lessons from this experience. He was still editing the film when Jonathan Taplin, the producer of *Mean Streets*, suggested that he film the farewell concert of The Band. Robbie Robertson's group, which had backed Bob Dylan and recorded some of the most important American rock albums of the 1960s, was due to give its final concert at San Francisco's Winterland at Thanksgiving 1976, before disbanding. Scorsese agreed to what should have been a simple 16mm project — and then he asked himself the question: 'But what if we tried to do something more elaborate?'[6] He asked the art director Boris Leven, a Hollywood veteran with whom he had just worked on *New York, New York*, to turn the 'garage' that was Winterland into a real concert venue. Leven hung chandeliers from the ceiling and borrowed a set from San Francisco Opera's *La Traviata*.

To avoid a pitfall that had dogged most filmed concerts previously — the cameras all running out of film at the same moment — he wrote a very detailed shooting script, using several 35mm cameras in turn and specifying the colour of the lighting.

The Last Waltz (1978) is the 'anti-*Woodstock*', and stakes rock and roll's claim to be considered great art. Seeing these musicians, who had become stars at the age of twenty and were now finally entering adulthood — The Band, Van Morrison, Eric Clapton — filmed seriously and with style, you're entirely convinced of it.

Musically and visually rich, *The Last Waltz* is the documentary counterpart of *New York, New York*. At this point in his career, Scorsese was more or less deliberately shooting a documentary to match each fiction film. Just after *Mean Streets*, he had made *Italianamerican* (1974), a portrait of Catherine and Charles Scorsese, a work of domestic intimacy and filial piety. The third documentary of this period, *American Boy: A Profile of Steven Prince* (1978) is a portrait of Scorsese's friend and collaborator, who captivates his audience. The 'boy' is funny and likeable, but he also describes how he emptied the magazine of an automatic weapon into a man and revived a heroin user by emptying a syringe of adrenalin into his heart, an anecdote that would later be used by Quentin Tarantino, in the screenplay of *Pulp Fiction* (1994). Unlike the first two, this documentary shot in 1978 preceded the fiction film with which it can be associated, *Raging Bull*, another descent into Hell, in the steps of Jake LaMotta, world heavyweight boxing champion from 1949 to 1951.

Opposite page (top to bottom): Neil Young, Ringo Starr, Bob Dylan and Van Morrison in *The Last Waltz* (1978).

Below: Martin Scorsese with Steven Prince on the set of *American Boy: A Profile of Steven Prince* (1978).

Robert De Niro in *Raging Bull* (1980).

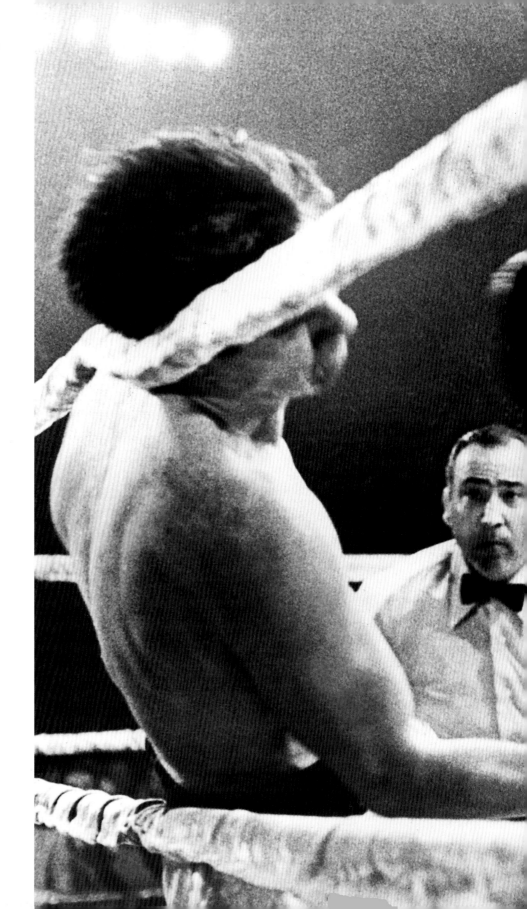

The boxing film: a Hollywood genre

When Martin Scorsese started working on *Raging Bull* in 1975, he seemed to be jumping onto a bandwagon. The boxing film was a sub-genre almost as old as Hollywood, and it enjoyed a spectacular renaissance in the 1970s, with Sylvester Stallone's triumph in *Rocky* in 1976. Scorsese isn't interested in boxing – he has said himself that he doesn't understand it at all.

Robert De Niro underwent a long period of training during the preparation of the film, and it was during one of his sessions that Scorsese saw an alternative to the prevailing Hollywood stereotypes about the ring. While De Niro was training, Scorsese would look the other way. Another experience helped him to work out the shot: when he attended some fights at Madison Square Garden, Scorsese, who had hardly any interest in the sport, was immediately struck by the image of a blood-soaked sponge that had fallen on the canvas. A little later, spectators in the front row were splashed with blood. 'And they call this

sport...,' he thought. Scorsese set about designing all the fights, giving them each a personality, from the apparent realism of the first confrontation between Jake LaMotta and Sugar Ray Robinson to the nightmare of their return bout, which has the forms, if not the colours, of a martyrdom painted in the late Middle Ages, with its fountains of blood spurting from the saint's wounds, and Robinson's grimacing, devilish expression that contrasts with LaMotta's mutilated features. The spectators and the ring have disappeared – the set was in fact twice the size of an actual ring – wreathed in smoke-effects. These excesses would probably be unbearable in colour. But during pre-production, Michael Powell, a veteran of British cinema and a great colourist – he made *The Red Shoes* (1948) – had remarked, 'These red gloves bother me', provoking a thought that led Scorsese to decide (and to insist on it to his producers) to shoot in black and white, which draws the excesses of the image towards

abstraction. Then came the editing and the soundtrack. For the edit, Scorsese and Thelma Schoonmaker based themselves on the rhythmic patterns he had experimented with in *The Last Waltz*. He also used the cutting to suggest the dislocation of space and the way a series of punches are perceived, as when he shows a punch delivered by Robinson and then dissolves to a shot of

LaMotta's legs, down which the blood is trickling.

Lastly, the soundtrack was created with Frank Warner, who developed new sounds, linked to the punches and the flash photography, and interrupting the highly organized cacophony with sudden periods of silence, which further heighten the impact of the chaos that will follow.

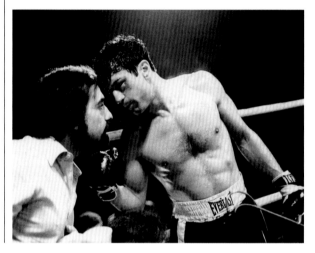

Martin Scorsese with Robert De Niro on the set of *Raging Bull* (1980).

Opposite page: Cathy Moriarty and Robert De Niro in *Raging Bull* (1980).

Raging Bull

Robert De Niro, who had already drawn Scorsese's attention to LaMotta's autobiography during the shooting of *Alice Doesn't Live Here Anymore*, brought it up again when his friend was at his lowest point. Scorsese, then living in a cocaine haze, neither took pleasure in the artistic success of *The Last Waltz* nor fully appreciated the depth of the failure of *New York, New York*. He half-heartedly accepted De Niro's proposal and worked on several versions of the screenplay, the last of which, by Paul Schrader, eventually captured his attention.

In the autumn of 1978, Scorsese suffered a serious health crisis. De Niro went to visit him in the hospital and asked him if he wanted to die. It was at that moment, he says, that 'I understood what Jake was, but only after having gone through a similar experience.'[7] At the opposite pole from sporting epics like *Rocky* (1976), which were starting to flood onto American screens, *Raging Bull* is a story of self-destruction.

On the island of Saint-Martin, De Niro and Scorsese rewrote the screenplay together. Then the actor turned himself into a boxer, spending hours in the ring. Later, in the summer of 1979, the shoot was suspended for three months while he put on the thirty kilos that would turn him into an ex-boxer. During the break, Scorsese married Isabella Rossellini, the daughter of one of his role models, Roberto Rossellini, and Ingrid Bergman.

For *Raging Bull*, Scorsese devised a new method of filming fights, and imposed his choice of black-and-white on the studio. During the shoot, a new dream couple came into being when Joe Pesci, who plays Jake LaMotta's brother, replaced Harvey Keitel opposite De Niro.

Raging Bull is considered today to be the pinnacle of Scorsese's work, but when it was released, some American critics greeted it with hostility, ac-cusing it of a violence decreasingly tolerated in Ronald Reagan's America, and denying the principal character the redemption that is in fact its central subject.

Its commercial failure was all the more painful since the film, which had been nominated for an Oscar, saw it snatched away by *Ordinary People* (1980), a family drama directed by Robert Redford, who also took the prize for best director, for which Scorsese was in the running. Scorsese realized at that moment that he was still not really a member of the Hollywood in-crowd. *Raging Bull* very soon took its place in lists of the best U.S. or world films, but its director's career seemed to have run into the buffers.

De Niro nevertheless won the Oscar for best actor, and Thelma Schoonmaker for best film editing. She had worked with Scorsese in the early days (although he had employed Marcia Lucas — the wife of the director of *Star Wars* — on his last three films) and she now rejoined him. Scorsese's collaboration with her has continued until the present.

Below: Robert De Niro in *The King of Comedy* (1983).

Opposite page: Jerry Lewis and Robert De Niro in *The King of Comedy* (1983).

The King of Comedy

The consequences of the commercial failure of *Raging Bull* were not felt right away. De Niro persuaded Scorsese to direct him again, this time in *The King of Comedy* (1982). Scorsese, who still had serious problems with his health and his use of drugs, was probably not the ideal person to direct a comedy, even a black one. The account of the persecution of a TV star, Jerry Lewis, by a mentally disturbed fan turned into a nightmare, on the set as much as on the screen. Of all his films, this is probably the one about which Scorsese has had the harshest things to say, and he may have regretted making one film too many with Robert De Niro. Nevertheless, even if it is often hard to watch, *The King of Comedy* is both a cruelly accurate satire on the world of celebrity, and — once again — the search for humanity in a character who appears to have none.

The film cost $18 million to make, but in the light of the first disastrous box-office results, 20th Century Fox, the distributors, decided to withdraw it from circulation.

'One film for me, one film for them'

From *After Hours* to *Casino*

Sharon Stone and Martin Scorsese
on the set of *Casino* (1995).

Right: Rosanna Arquette and
Griffin Dunne in *After Hours* (1985).

Following pages: Paul Newman in
The Color of Money (1986).

Early in 1983, as *The King of Comedy* was heading towards its commercial failure, Scorsese started work on a project that he had long cherished. According to Peter Biskind,[8] while they were shooting *Boxcar Bertha*, Barbara Hershey drew his attention to *The Last Temptation of Christ*, a novel by the Greek author Nikos Kazantzakis (1883–1957). Barry Diller and Michael Eisner, then in charge at Paramount, offered Scorsese the $12 million he needed.

Once again, the Catholic Scorsese turned to the Calvinist Paul Schrader for his screenplay. But Kazantzakis's novel had caused serious offence to all the Christian churches long before filming started. The story presents a human Christ, tempted even on the cross to renounce his divine nature and have children with Mary Magdalene. Outraged religious organizations began to put pressure on Gulf and Western, Paramount's mother company, to drop the project. When producers Irwin Winkler and Robert Chartoff went their separate ways, Jon Avnet agreed to continue with the film, but the pressure was too much in the end, and Paramount withdrew. Scorsese, however, did not give up. Two years later, the idea of producing it in Europe, with a significant French contribution, was mooted. This time, it was the bishops of the Catholic Church who put pressure on the French Socialist government to kill off the project.

For the moment, Scorsese made himself scarce; he returned to New York and shot a small-scale film, from a script offered to him by the actor Griffin Dunne. *After Hours* (1985), shot in New York within six weeks, served to demonstrate that he could carry through a project without going over the top.

He worked for the first time with the German cameraman Michael Ballhaus, who had previously worked with Fassbinder and could plan his shots very quickly, at a pace unfamiliar to Hollywood veterans. Scorsese would employ him six more times, from *The Color of Money* to *The Departed* (2006).

Scorsese made extensive changes to the screenplay of *After Hours*, which was in fact the graduation project of its author, Joseph Minion. The tribulations of Paul Hackett, a computer programmer whose night of adventure in SoHo turns into a nightmare, are like a cruelly mocking reflection of Scorsese's recent years. But instead of turning the film into a jeremiad, he gave it an unexpected youthful energy; never was a nightmare so much fun. On its U.S. release, and at Cannes, *After Hours* was hailed as evidence that Scorsese's career had taken off again.

The Color of Money

Scorsese was well aware that one independent film doesn't guarantee a fresh start. During the aborted preparation of *The Last Temptation of Christ*, he had been offered several commercial screenplays, including *Beverly Hills Cop* (Martin Brest, 1984). In the end, he agreed to make *The Color of Money* for Touchstone, a Disney subsidiary. Scorsese had decided to adopt King Vidor's motto: 'One film for me, one film for them.' *The Color of Money* would be made on the studio's terms, within the agreed time and budget.

The film was a sequel to *The Hustler* (which had been based on a novel by Walter Tevis and directed by Robert Rossen in 1961). It reintroduced the character of 'Fast Eddie' Felson, a virtuoso of the pool tables, played by Paul Newman, who was ready to repeat the role.

Scorsese didn't like the screenplay he was offered, and called on the novelist Richard Price, who had written about Italian-Americans. They both met with Newman and suggested turning Fast Eddie into a manipulative character who lives vicariously through young pool players. Newman was persuaded and the cast was completed with the arrival of Tom Cruise, who was not yet quite a superstar and wanted to prove he was also an actor. Although Scorsese's constant themes — corruption, betrayal — are still there, they are held at some distance by a plot that is too neatly worked out. But the film was completed on time, not all the budget

Paul Newman in Robert Rossen's *The Hustler* (1961).

Opposite page: Paul Newman and Tom Cruise in *The Color of Money* (1986).

was spent, and the public flocked to it. This time, Scorsese could face the future with confidence.

The Last Temptation of Christ

After Jon Avnet withdrew from the production of *The Last Temptation of Christ*, it was Scorsese's agent Harry Ufland who took up the reins. Early in 1987, Scorsese decided to transfer to another agent, Michael Ovitz, who was then on his way to becoming the most powerful man in Hollywood. Overnight, *The Last Temptation of Christ*, which had been the butt of jokes throughout the industry, became a viable project, and Universal agreed to finance it. Preparations started up again. Scenes shot in 1983, when the plan had been to shoot much of the film in Israel, had to be jettisoned, and in the end the choice of location fell on Morocco. For the role of Jesus, Aidan Quinn was replaced by Willem Dafoe, whom Scorsese

had noticed when he played a dealer in William Friedkin's *To Live and Die in L.A.* (1985).

In the excellent book *Scorsese on Scorsese*, a collection of interviews edited by Ian Christie and David Thompson, the pages devoted to *The Last Temptation of Christ* are among the most gripping. In them Scorsese reveals the intensity of his relationship with Catholicism, its rituals and beliefs, while at the same time systematically analysing it in cinematic terms. With an eye that is both sharp and charitable, he lists the great biblical films, including *The King of Kings*, formal and hieratic in Cecil B. DeMille's 1927 version, coarse and sensual in Nicholas Ray's of 1961, with Jeffrey Hunter. He analyses Max von Sydow's performance as Christ in John Huston's *The Bible* (1966) and delivers his fascinating thoughts on Pier Paolo Pasolini's *The Gospel According to Saint Matthew* (1964).

The Last Temptation of Christ
(1988).

Martin Scorsese on the set of *The Last Temptation of Christ* (1988).

Right: Paul Sorvino, Christopher Serrone, Joe Pesci, Robert De Niro and Joe D'Onofrio in *Goodfellas* (1990).

Following pages: Christopher Serrone, Joe D'Onofrio and Robert De Niro in *Goodfellas* (1990).

From his study of these films, Scorsese draws his own version of the Christ figure, whom he sees as being human so that his divinity may be truly put to the test on earth. This is the diametrical opposite of the psychopaths — Travis Bickle in *Taxi Driver* — or sociopaths — Nicky Santoro in *Casino* — to whom Scorsese always attributes a little humanity, in contrast with the hold over them of madness and evil.

Despite or because of the pain, work and love that went into its preparation and making, *The Last Temptation of Christ* is not the most successful of Scorsese's films. The screenplay tries to present a number of ambiguities, and is sometimes over-explicit. It is as if Scorsese had not always made a firm decision between the different approaches to directing he had learned from his study of cinema history. The result sometimes suggests one of those composite churches, each element of which is beautiful but which does not have an overall harmony. *The Last Temptation of Christ* is still a passionate, fascinating film, the work of a man who wants to draw the world's attention to a story it no longer listens to.

But the churches, and the Catholic Church first and foremost, were unable to acknowledge its merits, and its release, in the summer of 1988 in the United States, and in the autumn in Europe, was accompanied by a series of protests against it. The French bishops and their supporters were prominent in continuing to demand that the film be banned, but later had cause to regret the fact that a fundamentalist group set fire to a cinema in Paris's Latin Quarter, seriously injuring at least one member of the audience.

New York Stories, Goodfellas

Scorsese kept out of the controversy, merely deploring intolerance, and refusing to engage the censors in debate. In the summer of 1988, he had begun to shoot *Life Lessons*, a short lasting three-quarters of an hour, as his contribution to the ensemble film *New York Stories* (1989), the other directors being Woody Allen and Francis Ford Coppola. *Life Lessons* is based on Dostoevsky's *The Gambler*, and portrays a middle-aged painter at the height of his fame, played by Nick Nolte, who sees his girlfriend, played by Rosanna Arquette, growing apart from him. She is also a painter, and he has seduced her by inviting her to be his assistant. As in *New York, New York*, Scorsese exposes the quasi-electrical connections between sexual desire and artistic creativity.

In November 1988, André S. Labarthe filmed Scorsese for the French TV series *Cinéma, de notre temps*. In the episode called 'The Scorsese Machine', we see the director putting the last touches to the editing of *Life Lessons* and the pre-production of *Goodfellas* (1990). 55

He had moved his production company, which later went under the name Cappa — *from his mother's maiden name* — into the Brill Building, where all the big American publishers of pop music had their offices. The 'Scorsese machine' was a small, efficient organization, with its loyal members, first among them the editor, Thelma Schoonmaker, but also an archivist, whose job was study the TV schedules and record the films selected by Scorsese. Brian De Palma and Michael Powell used to stop by the office. But the Scorsese machine was above all Marty himself, with his amazing productivity, prodigious knowledge of cinema, and inexhaustible energy. At that time, he was also in demand as an actor; Bertrand Tavernier had him play the owner of a New York jazz club in *Round Midnight* in 1986. Three years later, Akira Kurosawa asked him to play Vincent van Gogh in one of his last films, *Dreams*. Later on, Scorsese made no more than brief, humorous appearances, often playing himself, the strangest of which is his transformation into a bearded fish in *Shark Tale*, an animated film produced by DreamWorks in 2004.

If the controversy surrounding *The Last Temptation of Christ* affected him he doesn't let it

Above, top: Martin Scorsese in Bertrand Tavernier's *'Round Midnight* (1986).

Above, bottom: Martin Scorsese in Akira Kurosawa's *Dreams* (1990).

Opposite page: Rosanna Arquette in *Life Lessons* (1989).

show in Labarthe's film. He talks about *Goodfellas* and about one of the projects that we have seen come and go throughout his career: a story about the arrival of Sicilian immigrants in the United States.

The following year was devoted to shooting *Goodfellas* and to its post-production. Scorsese had read a proof copy of Nicholas Pileggi's story about Henry Hill, a mafia 'pentito' (repentant), and he was sure he had found there an authentic voice through which to present organized crime. From the childhood in Queens of an Irish-American boy who dreams of being a gangster like the Italians, until his downfall, when he has to betray his associates and put himself under the protection of the Federal authorities, there was everything Scorsese needed: the need to belong and the fear of being excluded; the fragile boundary that separates the normal world from the world of monsters and treachery. Scorsese wrote the screenplay together with Pileggi, showing him some of the early Nouvelle Vague films, including *Breathless* (1960) and *Jules and Jim* (1962), so that Pileggi could adopt the narrative methods of Godard and Truffaut, with their sudden digressions and voice-over narrations that have the status of characters in their own right.

This disjointed narrative style enlarges apparently insignificant incidents and performs acrobatic twists and turns. The direction is like a distillation of Scorsese's accumulated experience: the virtuosity of the sequence-length shot that shows Henry Hill going into a nightclub through the kitchens; the psychotic violence of the big scene — a kind of obscene aria — when Joe Pesci beats up a young gangster for making a bad joke; the documentary exactness of the domestic scenes which show these gangsters as suburban Americans. And it takes to perfection Scorsese's method of creating original soundtracks. It contains the pillars of his rock pantheon, from 1950s vocal groups to the Rolling Stones. Sticking to his principle of not using sound for purposes of illustration, and his wish to intensify the emotional charge of his images, Scorsese uses 'Layla', by Eric Clapton's Derek and the Dominoes, in a macabre sequence.

For *Goodfellas*, Scorsese had the biggest budget of his career, $25 million. Taking $47 million in receipts, it did not equal the record of *The Color of Money* — $52.3 million — but it was still profitable.

Cape Fear

It was with *Cape Fear* that Scorsese briefly joined the club of directors whose work is profitable. It was a project he had inherited from his relationship with Universal Studios. In exchange for financing *The Last Temptation of Christ*, they offered him a number of commercial projects, including this remake of *Cape Fear*, an ultra-violent thriller first made in 1962 by Jack Lee Thompson. In it we see a criminal, Robert Mitchum, terrorizing his lawyer, played by Gregory Peck, and his family. This remake thus came into the category of films 'for them', and Scorsese carried it through without any major difficulties. Robert De Niro and Nick Nolte took the roles previously played by Mitchum and Peck, both of whom also appear in the film in minor roles.

The allusions to other films in *Cape Fear* are unobtrusive, and by and large Scorsese abides by the rules of the Hollywood 'terror film' as it has been made since the early 1990s. De Niro appears very much to enjoy being terrifying — the role demands it,

Robert De Niro and Nick Nolte in *Cape Fear* (1991).

Opposite page: Daniel Day-Lewis and Michelle Pfeiffer in *The Age of Innocence* (1993).

Following pages: Winona Ryder and Daniel Day-Lewis in *The Age of Innocence* (1993).

of course — but as a result he is much less so than in the past. The final sequence has on one side the persecuted family, forced to become killers, and on the other, the murderer who is about to become a victim. The action takes place on the southeast coast of the United States, allowing De Niro to try out a new accent and Wesley Strick, the screenwriter, to set his bloody conclusion in the midst of a hurricane. Scorsese used the opportunity of this meteorological event to bone up on the latest innovations in special effects.

The film's noticeable conformism and the over-elaborate way in which Scorsese disguises his themes — the family's ultimate redemption, the complexity of the relationship between crime and religion — did not prevent *Cape Fear* doing extremely well in cinemas (rather the contrary), taking $79 million in receipts in North America alone. For once, Scorsese had two popular successes one after the other, and his standing with the studios was at its highest.

The Age of Innocence

Cappa Productions now became a real company. Scorsese had met the producer Barbara De Fina while he was making *After Hours* and had married her. She has produced all his films since *The Color of Money*, and she also supports him in his activity as a producer. He had backed Stephen Frears for *The Grifters* (1990) and now produced John McNaughton's *Mad Dog and Glory* (1993), starring Bill Murray and De Niro.

When Fox dropped him at the last moment over one of the projects dearest to his heart, he returned without any regrets to Columbia, who agreed to finance *The Age of Innocence*. Jay Cocks, a long-time friend, critic and co-scriptwriter of *Raging Bull* and *The Last Temptation of Christ*, had given him Edith Wharton's novel in 1980, insisting that the book 'was him', was Scorsese. The relationship between the son of working-class Italian-Americans and Newland Archer, the scion of a New York dynasty in the late nineteenth century, is not immediately

Above, top: Farley Granger and Alida Valli in Luchino Visconti's *Senso* (1954).

Above, bottom: Katharina Renn and Fernand Fabre in Roberto Rossellini's *The Taking of Power by Louis XIV* (1966).

clear. Published in 1920 by the sixty-eight-year-old Edith Wharton, *The Age of Innocence* brings back to life a society long-vanished even then, as it describes the unconsummated love affair between Archer and his cousin, the Countess Olenska, who owes her name to a disastrous European marriage. Archer, who is engaged to an exquisite young woman, May Welland, never succeeds in acting on his feelings, crushed by pressure from his peers.

Henry Hill, the Irish gangster who dreamed of being Italian, never managed to force his entry into a community he idealized. Newland Archer, the New York lawyer, cannot break down the door of a prison he longs to escape. For Scorsese, this was also the moment to show he could pass the test of the costume film, and win a place beside Visconti's *Senso* (1954) and *The Leopard* (1963), William Wyler's *The Heiress* (1949), and Rossellini's *The Taking of Power by Louis XIV* (1967), all films he mentioned in interviews he gave when *The Age of Innocence* was released.

For the part of Newland Archer, he drew on the services of Daniel Day-Lewis, the young British actor introduced by Stephen Frears in *My Beautiful Laundrette* (1984) and by James Ivory in *A Room with a View* (1986). Michelle Pfeiffer (Countess Olenska) and Winona Ryder (May Welland) completed the cast. With Michael Ballhaus as cameraman, in March 1992 Scorsese began to direct Edith Wharton's harsh story. He paid fanatical attention to historical detail, turning himself into an historian of the eating habits of New York's high society and a fine connoisseur of etiquette and protocol. This quasi-documentary obsession takes him to the inner truth of his characters, and Scorsese obtained miracles of restraint from his cast.

Camera movements in clearly defined spaces trace the lines of sexual desire and social convention, until the accumulation of these barriers builds the tomb in which Newland Archer's dreams are buried.

But *The Age of Innocence* cannot be reduced merely to the cruelty of Edith Wharton's novel. Scorsese takes such delight in filming these people, and these costumes, objects and settings, that the film often seems to forget to be unhappy. It borrows from Michael Powell and Emeric Pressburger, and develops, the idea of colour dissolves: instead of fading to black, a shot explodes into red, yellow or rust. The effect of sumptuousness is never

Thelma Schoonmaker, editor

Do you read the screenplay before shooting and editing?

Yes, I read it first, but then I try to forget it because I like to get a feel of the film through the rushes they send me regularly during shooting. I want to see what Marty's filming, and to respond only to that. With him, the screenplay doesn't really reflect what he's going to do. His films are always more complex and profound than his screenplays. He adds details, atmosphere. *Goodfellas* is a very 'tight' screenplay, because he had worked on it for two years, and the book had already been written. I think by the time we finished we had cut only one scene: the one in which the little boy learns to drink espressos. We cut much more in *Casino*. Research and documentation continued while we were shooting. They changed a lot of things while they were filming. ... It was harder to control than *Goodfellas*, for which the story was more straightforward.

How does his style influence your work? Does he use longer shots or does he prefer very short ones? When he's filming is he already thinking about the editing stage?

He likes to experiment, to go in a specific direction with each new project ... My style of editing is in fact his ... For the last four or five films, he has focused on the movement from objective to subjective shots. A shot appears to be shown from a particular point of view, and then the character comes into the shot, which becomes a simple shot of him, even to the point where you then go back to a subjective shot. He makes more and more elaborate experiments on the basis of this principle.

This is an extract from an interview with Nicolas Saada, published in *Cahiers du cinéma*, no. 500, March 1996.

Thelma Schoomaker in 1996.

oppressive, because we are easily persuaded that it springs from the joy of an outsider able at last to stake his claim to the things that were furthest from the reach of the huddled masses who thronged the immigration desks of Ellis Island.

    The Age of Innocence was presented at the Venice Film Festival in 1993, a few days after the death of Charles Scorsese, to whom it is dedicated.

A journey through American movies

A Personal Journey with Martin Scorsese Through American Movies, commissioned by the British TV company Channel Four, continues the thoughtful, almost contemplative, humour of *The Age of Innocence*. In a little under four hours, Scorsese, who wrote the screenplay with Michael Henry Wilson, strolls through the cinema's first hundred years, rather than writing its history. The very title, *A Personal Journey with Martin Scorsese Through American Movies*, an itinerary in the first person, reveals its subjective point of view. As well as addressing aesthetic issues, Scorsese is intent on tracing the demarcation line between art and commerce that runs through the Hollywood system. And the question was an urgent one for him. Since making *The Color of Money* Scorsese had been able to go from one studio to another, using as his 'pilot fish' the most influential of Hollywood power players, his agent, Michael Ovitz. But Ovitz had decided to go over to the studios' camp and was preparing to join Michael Eisner at Disney. In 1995, he took Scorsese with him, but before he could sign an agreement with Disney and act on it, Scorsese still owed Universal one film, under the contract between the company and Cappa.

Casino

This film would be *Casino*, another gangster movie that on the face of it seems like a repeat of *Goodfellas*. The leading roles were taken by Robert De Niro and Joe Pesci. They play two gangsters, one Jewish, the other Italian, whose job is to take control of the Las Vegas casinos on behalf of the Chicago mob. The screenplay was again based on facts unearthed by Nicholas Pileggi, and the original soundtrack was once more a compilation, this time mixing Bach with the inevitable Rolling Stones.

In fact, *Casino* is the antithesis of *Goodfellas*. The vitality of petty criminals who aspire to material success gives way to the story of a long agony that links the decline of 1960s Las Vegas to the disintegration of a marriage. Almost twenty years after *New York, New York*, the role of Sam Rothstein again puts De Niro in artificial sets where he has to perform a fatal courtship dance. Liza Minnelli has been replaced by Sharon Stone. Basking in the success of *Basic Instinct* (1992), she finds in the character of Ginger, a girl who lives by her wits and wins power and money through her affair with Sam Rothstein, the one great role of her career.

In the impressively ugly sets that look as though they have escaped from the 1960s, the film sucks its despicable characters into a maelstrom of violence and lies that doesn't even end in apocalypse, but just an accumulation of violent deaths and, what's even worse, defeats. *Casino* is not, then, an exhilarating film. It runs for almost three hours, and when U.S. cinema managers saw it at a trade event, the ShowEast, in November 1995, most of them left the auditorium well before the end of the film.

It had cost a lot of money, over $60 million. At the time, Hollywood budgets were soaring and would soon pass the $100 million mark. As Ron Meyer, the new boss of Universal, pointed out, a responsible director cannot invest such sums without being confident of recovering his expenses.

Opposite and following pages:

Sharon Stone in *Casino* (1995).

Return to New York

From *Kundun* to *The Departed*

Cameron Diaz and Leonardo DiCaprio
in *Gangs of New York* (2002).

In 1995, Martin Scorsese arrived at the home of Mickey Mouse. In August of the same year, his agent, Michael Ovitz, became president of Disney, a post he held for only sixteen months before being unceremoniously dismissed by his co-president, Michael Eisner, the man who, at Paramount, had bowed to fundamentalist pressure and dropped *The Last Temptation of Christ*.

It was perhaps as some kind of expiation that Eisner agreed to finance *Kundun* (1997), a story about the youth of the Dalai Lama, from his recognition as the incarnation of the Buddha, at the age of five, to the Chinese invasion of Tibet in 1959. The screenplay was offered to Scorsese by Melissa Mathison, who had written *E.T.* (1982) and is herself a Buddhist. For his part, Ovitz promised Disney he would smooth over any problems with the Chinese authorities, at a time when the studio had its eye on a promising market.

The result was that in 1996 Scorsese again found himself in the mountains of Morocco, nine years after he made *The Last Temptation of Christ*. Most of the non-professional roles were filled by an exclusively Tibetan cast, and a reconstruction of the Potala, an historic palace of the Dalai Lama in Lhasa, was built in the Atlas mountains.

With the exception of a few moments, *Kundun* is as smooth as *The Last Temptation of Christ* was tormented, something that probably had to do with the nature of the two spiritualities involved. One can feel that Scorsese was moved by the story of the Dalai Lama's early years in Lhasa, the life of a child snatched from his home, living among strangers, who observes the world from the bedroom that he is unable to leave. Because these people's ways of being and of speaking are even more interiorized and coded than those of the New York aristocrats of *The Age of Innocence*, for the first time Scorsese used a number of elaborate, violent dream sequences to evoke the inner torment of his principal character.

On the other hand, the conflict between Tibet and China is treated superficially. Scorsese had never dealt directly with political issues, and his approach smacks of mistrust and a lack of self confidence. Just when shooting was finished, in January 1997, Catherine Scorsese died. Her son, who had followed her final months of illness from the set of *Kundun* in Morocco, was at her side in New York.

When it was released in December 1997, the film, which had angered the Chinese authorities, was poorly distributed and took only $6 million dollars in receipts, whereas it had cost $26 million.

Bringing Out the Dead

In 1998, the year in which he chaired the jury at Cannes, Scorsese worked unsuccessfully on a biography of the crooner Dean Martin, from which Nicholas Pileggi was to write a screenplay. He then pounced on an autobiographical novel written by a New York ambulance driver, Joe Connelly, who had taken his title, *Bring Out Your Dead*, from Monty Python, referring to the epidemic of plague in *Monty Python and the Holy Grail* (Terry Jones and Terry Gilliam, 1975).

Bringing Out the Dead (1999) is set in New York, in the early 1990s, at the height of the social and financial crisis that rocked the city. If we bear in mind that *Goodfellas* took place for the most part in the suburbs, and *The Age of Innocence* in a city that has now almost completely disappeared, *Bringing Out the Dead* marks for Scorsese a return to Manhattan, to the city in which he grew up, and where he became a director.

Everything in the film takes us back to *Taxi Driver*. First of all, Scorsese asked Paul Schrader to write the screenplay. And the main character drives up and down the streets of Manhattan, observing all the evidence of its decline and decay.

But *Bringing Out the Dead* tells another story altogether. Frank Pierce, the strange hero played by Nicolas Cage, is the almost exact antithesis of Travis Bickle. The taxi driver was defeated by the nightmare of the city, while Frank has only a single wish, to wake up from it, and to escape. The Christian imagery of *Taxi Driver* had to do with mortification and sacrifice, yet was never presented as such. This time, Scorsese puts his cards on the table: the action takes place from Thursday to Friday, like Christ's passion. With its two Madonnas, the ghost of a drug addict, and Mary, played by Patricia Arquette, *Bringing Out the Dead* is like an album of religious images, a feeling that is reinforced by the soundtrack, which is made up partly of pop songs whose words coincide with those of the liturgy or chapters of the Bible: 'Too Many Fish In The Sea', by the Marvelettes, and 'Red Red Wine', by UB40.

The film is full of macabre humour that has nothing in common with the sadism prevalent in American cinema at the time. The sight of a gangster impaled on railings is simply odd, just one more vision in Frank Pierce's half-awakened world, directed by Scorsese with a kind of compassionate detachment, as if the spiritual lessons of *Kundun* were now bearing fruit.

The film was produced by Disney, and was a partial failure, but that was not enough to break the link between the director and the company. In fact, Miramax, the New York studio set up by brothers Bob and Harvey Weinstein and acquired by Disney in 1993, was ready to support a project that Scorsese had had in mind for over of twenty years.

Gangs of New York

Gangs of New York had been announced as early as 1977 in *Variety*, the official organ of the Hollywood film industry. At that time, it was Sergio Leone's producer, Alberto Grimaldi, who was going to make it.

Scorsese got the idea to make this film when he read Herbert Asbury's *The Gangs of New York*. Written in 1928, it is one of the first attempts to tell the story of the other America, the America of organized crime and intercommunal conflict, in this case the resistance by 'native-born Americans' to Irish immigration in the mid-nineteenth century.

Opposite page, top: Martin Scorsese and Roberto Benigni in Cannes in 1998.

Opposite page, bottom: Nicolas Cage in *Bringing Out the Dead* (1999).

Below: John Goodman and Nicolas Cage in *Bringing Out the Dead* (1999).

From Robert to Leonardo

Robert De Niro appears in only eight of the twenty feature films made by Martin Scorsese and plays the lead in only six of them. Nevertheless, no actor in cinema history has been so closely associated with a director, that privilege usually being reserved for actresses – Marlene Dietrich and Josef von Sternberg, for example. Beginning with *Mean Streets*, Robert De Niro has embodied Scorsese's style. His acting is a product of the Actors Studio, involving immersion in the character and a search for his or her emotions. But it is less explanatory, more opaque, than that of his elders, Montgomery Clift, Marlon Brando or James Dean. During the making of *Mean Streets* and *Taxi Driver*, Scorsese developed with De Niro a method that involved the actor in building the character, even if the screenplay had to be changed

as a result of this approach. The director always applies this method with his actors, as was recently confirmed by Vera Farmiga, the female lead of *The Departed*.

With De Niro, this communication became so close that they hardly needed to use words, to the point, sometimes, of irritating the other actors. With Scorsese, De Niro can risk everything. He never defends a character, never tries to be charming, as Nicholson can, or to arouse sympathy, like Dustin Hoffmann. The high point of their collaboration remains to this day *Raging Bull*, in which Robert De Niro accomplishes a physical feat, altering his external appearance to fit the vicissitudes of his character's life, but above all, succeeds in plumbing the depths of a soul whose existence we had barely suspected.

Later, in *Cape Fear*, a project that he brought to Scorsese, De Niro dares to go to the extreme, and, as if fascinated, the director allows him to do so, even at the expense of the film. That situation was later repeated twice. In *Gangs of New York*, Daniel Day-Lewis, who plays Bill the Butcher – a role originally envisaged for De Niro – adopts an acting style close to mime, at the opposite pole from the extreme restraint he had shown in *The Age of Innocence*. In *The Departed*, Jack Nicholson makes the character of Frank Costello exist in a space of his own, slightly apart from the rest of the film, like a sort of operatic stage, while the other characters move in film noir settings.

The Departed also marks the maturity of the collaboration between Scorsese and Leonardo DiCaprio. The young actor had

played a slightly transparent avenger in *Gangs of New York* and had not always been able to give substance to the psychoses and megalomania of multi-millionaire Howard Hughes in *The Aviator*. As an undercover police officer, he is gripping in his tension and vulnerability, and it is he who gives humanity to the Hell of *The Departed*.

Scorsese may have been loyal to a number of actors, but he has been much more fickle with his actresses. This is not to say that he underemploys them: Ellen Burstyn, in *Alice Doesn't Live Here Anymore*, Liza Minnelli, in *New York, New York*, Rosanna Arquette, in *After Hours*, Michelle Pfeiffer and Winona Ryder, in *The Age of Innocence*, Sharon Stone, in *Casino*, and Cate Blanchett, in *The Aviator*, are all indebted to him for some of their finest roles.

Below, left: Robert De Niro in *Raging Bull* (1980).

Below, right: Leonardo DiCaprio in *The Aviator* (2004).

Opposite page: Leonardo DiCaprio in *Gangs of New York* (2002).

Following pages: Cameron Diaz, Daniel Day-Lewis and Leonardo DiCaprio in *Gangs of New York* (2002).

This war was played out in the Five Points, a neigh-bourhood in lower Manhattan, on the site of today's Chinatown, and not far from Little Italy.

With Jay Cocks, Scorsese wrote nine versions of the first screenplay, telling a story of revenge taken by Amsterdam Vallon, the son of an Irish gang-leader killed by Bill 'The Butcher' Poole, who leads a gang of 'Natives'. He still needed an actor to play Amsterdam, because De Niro had agreed to play Bill. After he left Disney, Ovitz had set up another agency. His associate, Rick Yorn, was man-aging the career of Leonardo DiCaprio, a global star since his role in *Titanic* (1997). The young actor, who was then shooting *The Beach* (1998), accepted the part with enthusiasm, and work on *Gangs of New York* could finally begin.

It was an enormous project, and required the construction of countless sets and the use of hun-dreds of extras. An initial budget was set at $84 mil-lion. Harvey Weinstein, one of the two founders of Miramax, is a producer of a kind that Scorsese had never encountered before. He intervenes at every stage in the making of a film, but his preferred tech-nique is to take possession of the material already shot and to oversee the editing himself.

No doubt to protect himself from excessive interference, Scorsese had drawn on other sources of funding. It was the young British producer Graham King, whom Scorsese would call upon again for *The Aviator* (2004) and *The Departed*, who raised most of the money, by selling the film rights on the international market. Weinstein had arranged for

Steven Zaillian, who wrote the scripts for *Schindler's List* (1993) and *Hannibal* (2001), to take over the screenplay. Zaillian set the confrontation between Amsterdam Vallon and Bill the Butcher in its historical context, the grip of the Democratic party machine on New York and the anti-conscription riots provoked by the American Civil War. After Robert De Niro's withdrawal, Scorsese persuaded Daniel Day-Lewis to emerge from reclusive life and take on the role of Bill the Butcher.

Just before he started filming, on sets built at the Cinecittà studio in Rome, Scorsese presented at the Venice Festival, a year late, *My Voyage to Italy*, which had originally been intended to close the 1999 festival. While *A Personal Journey with Martin Scorsese Through American Movies* was an autobiography of the man and of the artist through his discovery of films, this stroll through the two decades that took Italian cinema from neo-realism to the great films of Fellini and Antonioni

seems more like an act of homage to great filmmakers who are perhaps revered more than they are loved. The film consists of very long extracts, a bit like a literature textbook, and Scorsese made it out of a feeling of anxiety that some of the films presented might disappear completely. He said, 'I had almost lost hope that one day we might see [Rossellini's] *Viaggio in Italia* or *Europa 51* in good copies.'[9] The film was also designed to give audiences without access to these works an idea of their importance and impact.

Before the first day's filming, the budget for *Gangs of New York* had already reached $93 million. The shoot began in September 2000 and lasted seven months, two more than anticipated. On the set, the first confrontations between Weinstein and Scorsese were violent. The producer objected to Daniel Day-Lewis's physical appearance — blind in one eye and with a moustache — which he thought would hamper the publicity campaign.

Martin Scorsese in his own words

When you spoke at the Cinémathèque française, you said that the theatrical release of a movie was now just a small part of its life. In what way has it changed your work as a filmmaker?

It has changed in the sense that at this stage we're aiming the post-production more towards the DVD release. Of course, there is the film, there is completing the actual film, but the DVD is as important and maybe becoming more important that the actual release of the projected film. Now the film may be in the future digitally projected and that's something else entirely too. We find that the production of the DVD is a burden because the DVD audience expects many extras. And the extras are becoming conventional extras, for instance, 'the making of'.

Who are they aimed at?

There appears to be a new level of film viewers who are interested exclusively in technology rather than the film itself. What I mean by that is what the film says.

You mean people who are interested just in the special effects?

And also it seems to me that the more fantastic a film is, the more technology is used in terms of special effects, the more this new group wants to see how the effect was achieved and therefore it loses the magic, the mystery of the cinema.

When you discovered cinema, did you have no interest in the way it was done?

Sometimes we talked about it, but not very much. It was always the reaction to the film itself, the overall impact of the film. When I did the airplane scenes in *Aviator*, I realized what William Wellman did, what Howard Hawks did, what Griffith did, what Thomas Ince, Abel Gance, what so many extraordinary people did at the beginning of cinema. You don't know until you physically get up there and try to deal with the elements and try to understand the extraordinary miracle that was being invented every day at the beginning of the cinema.

So what is being invented nowadays through digital technology is not of the same nature?

No, but that doesn't mean it's bad. It all depends on what you want to say. As long as it deals with something that is human, with our humanity rather than something that is, how should I say, empty, nihilistic. This could be a problem culturally around the world, in the Western world no doubt. It reminds me of the bread and circuses of ancient Rome. If you imagine the spectacles that were being put on in the Coliseums of the ancient world, the level of production, spectacle. Now compare that to some of the plays of the Greek playwrights that were being performed. You can't deny the value of the spectacle in the Roman Coliseum in which thousands of animals were slaughtered and people were killed, as opposed to the Theban cycle of Sophocles.

When films are digitally shot and digitally screened, what will constitute the true work?

When you lose the 35mm print, you can do what you want with a movie. There are now on American TV commercials where the images of characters from old movies or TV shows are right there and they're speaking. I know that they're not speaking, that someone is imitating them and that a machine is making sound like that, and it's their image, and the lipsinc is perfect. You can manipulate the image any way you want.

Up to now, the great filmmakers have been about human beings. That's what I'm worried about, Can you not create a digital image of a human being and create a film that is about human beings, maybe, that's a possibility. In a sense, we're not too far away from what Walt Disney was doing. I like Walt Disney, but quite honestly I can't watch those films. I have a child now, we show her the films, they are quite beautiful, amazing but as an adult you need more than Snow White, Bambi and Dumbo, you simply do. No matter how extraordinary the animation is and how true to human nature, I prefer films about people.

This is an extract from an interview with Thomas Sotinel published in *Le Monde*, 28 November 2005.

Opposite page: Daniel Day-Lewis in *Gangs of New York* (2002).

But that was nothing in comparison with the guerrilla warfare between the two men during post-production. To his great frustration, Weinstein realized he could do nothing against the alliance of Scorsese and Schoonmaker. But Scorsese still complained about Weinstein's interference, and he sees it as one of the reasons behind the film's imperfections.

And it's true that, like another long-cherished project, *The Last Temptation of Christ*, *Gangs of New York* is a failure. A magnificent failure, of course, but the screenplay does not succeed in giving overall coherence to the film's different levels, individual and collective, communal and political, melodramatic and historical. Yet, while it may not have a place among Scorsese's great films, *Gangs of New York* is of crucial importance in his body of work. It was at this point that he attempted to give an historical form to all the anxieties, all the political questions, that underlie his films: who is really an American?

On what values does the unity of the nation rest? The almost ethnological approach of *Mean Streets* or *Goodfellas* gives way to epic, and when the film attains this dimension — as in the initial confrontation between the 'Natives' and the 'Dead Rabbits', the Irish gang — we see clearly the outlines of the heroic canvas to which Scorsese was aspiring.

The attacks of 11 September 2001 came in the middle of editing. The film, which should have been ready by the end of the year, so that it could compete for an Oscar, was delayed. Scorsese and Weinstein agreed that this was not the moment to show New York in flames. *Gangs of New York* was finally released in December 2002, in time for the following year's Oscars campaign.

Of all the studios, Miramax was best placed to do everything necessary if the film was to carry away a statuette. But this year, the Weinstein brothers' company had another serious candidate, the musical *Chicago*. And Harvey Weinstein wasn't shy about making it known that Rob Marshall, the director of *Chicago*, had been much more compliant than Scorsese when it came to changes in the editing of his film. As it turned out, it was *Chicago* that won its Oscars: once again, Scorsese went home empty-handed.

The Aviator and Feel Like Going Home

Through Graham King, who had worked with Michael Mann on the production of *Ali* (2001), Scorsese inherited a project originally intended for the director of *Collateral* (2004). *The Aviator* was a biography of the multi-millionaire Howard Hughes, in which Leonardo DiCaprio was to play the lead. A commissioned film as expensive as *Gangs of New York*, it was again co-financed by Graham King and Harvey Weinstein, with additional support from Warner Bros. This time, the shoot, which involved aerial sequences that were very difficult to handle, went more smoothly. Scorsese emerged from it feeling elated.

And since Howard Hughes, not content with being a pioneer aviator, was also a producer during the Golden Age of Hollywood, *The Aviator* was also the first of Scorsese's fiction films to deal with the subject of cinema. In the roles of legendary stars he cast actors and actresses who bore only a distant resemblance to their models: Kate Beckinsale as Ava Gardner, Jude Law as Errol Flynn, Gwen Stefani as Jean Harlow and — a brilliant stroke — Cate

Kate Beckinsale (top), Leonardo DiCaprio and Gwen Stefani (bottom) in *The Aviator* (2004).

Opposite page: Martin Scorsese with Leonardo DiCaprio on the set of *The Aviator* (2004).

Blanchett as Katharine Hepburn. Scorsese, who had helped to destroy the star system with Robert De Niro, and then to rebuild it with Leonardo DiCaprio, had great fun playing games with these simulacra of the 'old' Hollywood.

The film's nimble pace and Bob Richardson's lush images certainly make *The Aviator* a much more enjoyable film than *Gangs of New York*, but the central figure of Howard Hughes remains veiled beneath a smooth performance by Leonardo DiCaprio, who revels in certain dramatic conventions of American cinema – the air crash, the appearance before a Congressional committee – while never putting across the madness and excess of the character he is playing. Granted, the film was snubbed again at the Oscars, but it was a success at the box office, the biggest of Scorsese's

career, taking $213 million in receipts worldwide. Scorsese regained his huge appetite for work. He had agreed to produce a series of seven films for TV on the blues and, when Spike Lee abandoned the project he was working on, Scorsese took over *Feel Like Going Home: The Blues from Africa to the New World* (2003). This search for the African roots of the blues is actually an assemblage of disparate elements, few of which were shot by Scorsese, but he could pride himself on having directed the most moving sequence, which shows a fife player from Mississippi, Otha Turner, the last exponent of the music played by African slaves when they landed in America. Scorsese has captured here a concrete trace of the origins of the American social contract, the very thing he had tried to put on the screen in *Gangs of New York*.

No Direction Home, The Departed

In the autumn of 2005, Scorsese presented *No Direction Home*, a documentary about Bob Dylan, at the Toronto Festival. He had just finished shooting *The Departed*, a film noir with, again, Leonardo DiCaprio.

 No Direction Home and *The Departed* are, each in its own way, a return to Scorsese's formative years, and he seems both horrified and filled with wonder. Wonder shines through the film on Dylan, none of which Scorsese shot himself. Jeff Rosen, the manager of the writer of 'Like A Rolling Stone', gave him material that included old films — mostly those made by D. A. Pennebaker — and more recent interviews with Dylan and his contemporaries.

 The skill of Scorsese and, as usual, of Thelma Schoonmaker, was to organize this mass of images and music so as to tell the story of the tremendous misunderstanding that had developed between the public and a deeply individualist artist promoted to the role of prophet for his generation. The deeply

ambiguous figure of Dylan becomes, through the editing alone, a Scorsese character, a Christ-like figure who aspires to humanity, a *monstre sacré* about whom we no longer know what has created him, world-wide adulation or his own genius.

 The Departed is also built around a monstrous figure, that of Frank Costello, an Irish gangster played by Jack Nicholson. The film's prologue, lasting only a few minutes, which describes the race riots in Boston in the 1970s, against the soundtrack of the Rolling Stones' 'Gimme Shelter', is a cruel account of failure, showing how much more divided American society became after the convulsions of the decade from 1965 to 1975. *The Departed* is certainly Martin Scorsese's most political film, but this aspect is hidden under a virtuoso screenplay. The film is a remake of *Infernal Affairs* (2004), an excellent Hong Kong thriller made by Alan Mak and Andy Lau. Leonardo DiCaprio and Matt Damon take the roles played by Tony Leung and Andy Lau, as two young

Leonardo DiCaprio in *The Aviator* (2004).

Right: Matt Damon in *The Departed* (2006).

Following pages: Martin Scorsese with Leonardo
DiCaprio on the set of *The Departed* (2006).

police officers, one sent by the authorities to infiltrate the world of organized crime, the other having entered the police force on behalf of the mob.

For the first time, Scorsese portrays police officers, the first time he rubs up against an agency of government, and this friction generates an electrical charge that runs right through the film. Opposite Jack Nicholson's flamboyant performance, and Matt Damon's icy opacity, Leonardo DiCaprio at last succeeds in showing his mettle and is heart-rending in his character of a masochistic martyr who plunges ever deeper into his clandestine existence while being increasingly convinced that his mission is futile.

All over the world, *The Departed* was an unprecedented commercial success for Scorsese, taking $288 million in box-office receipts. But most important of all, it finally gave him the single honour he had so long been denied: in February 2007, he at last won the Oscar for best director, while his co-producer Graham King received the award for best film. On the evening of the ceremony, Scorsese pretended not to believe his good fortune, and asked somebody to check the envelope. But the statuette was destined to be his; he was officially a great man, and he could give himself a little break.

Below: Leonardo DiCaprio and Jack Nicholson in *The Departed* (2006).

Opposite page: Martin Scorsese with Jack Nicholson on the set of *The Departed* (2006).

Show Business and Terror

From *Shine a Light* to *Shutter Island*

Christina Aguilera, Mick Jagger and Keith Richards in *Shine A Light* (2008).

Following pages: The Rolling Stones with Buddy Guy in *Shine A Light* (2008).

Pages 92–3: Mark Ruffalo and Leonardo DiCaprio in *Shutter Island* (2010).

A late meeting

In autumn 2006, Scorsese filmed two concerts by the Rolling Stones, who had previously been heard on the soundtrack of *Mean Streets*. For two evenings, the Stones exchanged the venues where they were performing for the Beacon Theatre, one of the most attractive in Manhattan. Repeating the pattern of *The Last Waltz*, Scorsese used several cameras, determined to miss none of Mick Jagger's grimaces or Keith Richards's wrinkles.

We had to wait eighteen months to see *Shine a Light* (2008; the title is taken from a little-known Stones song, buried on the fourth side of *Exile On Main Street*), which was presented at the 2008 Berlin International Film Festival, in February. The end result is an odd piece of work, scarcely a documentary at all. At the beginning of *Shine a Light*, Scorsese and Jagger pretend to argue about the excessive number of cameras, which threaten to obstruct the rock star's gyrations. As they explained at the press conference they held in Berlin, these exchanges were all scripted in advance of filming.

The shots outside the Beacon Theatre are digitally manipulated, and the audience at the concert was hand-picked, not according to the fans' enthusiasm, but more in terms of the women's measurements. All things considered, *Shine a Light* is Scorsese's only pure comedy. Whereas *The Last Waltz*, which showed a group of young musicians on the point of splitting up, was imbued with a deep melancholy, the sixty-something Scorsese observes his rocker contemporaries with a mixture of irony — he is taken in by neither Jagger's prima donna antics nor Keith Richards's pose as an old rebel — and admiration: as we both see and hear, the Stones are still a very good rock group.

In the same laid-back spirit, Scorsese accepted the overtures of a Spanish advertising agency, one of whose clients was the cava-maker Freixenet. The result, rather than a pure commercial, was a short film, *The Key to Reserva* (2007), which is both a 'story within a story' and a pastiche. A story within a story because, as in *Shine a Light*, the director includes himself in the action, this time in the role of a disciple overwhelmed at discovering a solitary page from a lost screenplay attributed to Alfred Hitchcock. We see Scorsese announcing his intention to shoot this fragment, and the latter part of the film consists of this pastiche. Inspired by both *Notorious* (1946; it involves a bottle that can only be reached by means of an inaccessible key) and *The Man Who Knew Too Much* (1956; the action takes place at a symphony

concert), *The Key to Reserva* is a *jeu d'esprit* on the joys of making films, when one is walking in the footsteps of one's mighty predecessors.

Shutter Island

Following *The Departed*, it was expected that Scorsese, who was said to be tired of working with the big studios, would finally devote himself to the project he has often said is closest to his heart: an adaptation of *Chinmoku*, the 1966 novel by the Japanese author Shusaku Endo (its English title is *Silence*), which describes the fate of a renegade seventeenth-century Catholic priest at the time when Christians were being persecuted in imperial Japan. But Paramount wished to capitalize on the success of *The Departed*, and persuaded Scorsese to adapt *Shutter Island* (2010), a 2003 bestseller by the Boston thriller-writer, Dennis Lehane, the author of *Mystic River*, which had been adapted by Clint Eastwood in 2003.

The story is set in 1954, in Boston, the same city as *The Departed*. Scorsese again cast Leonardo DiCaprio, who by now had a good command of the local accent. He plays Teddy Daniels, a federal agent tasked with investigating a psychiatric hospital for the criminally insane, built on a island in Boston Bay. The young Argentinian director Celina Murga published, in *Cahiers du cinéma* (no. 641, January 2009), a rare account of the shoot, which took place in the spring and early summer of 2008. She was attached to Scorsese as part of a mentoring programme sponsored by a leading brand of clocks and watches and was able to observe his working methods closely. She describes a director who thinks on the set in terms of the editing, his first concern being the position of a shot in the overall organization of the film, directing his actors' faces in relation to the following reverse shot, and making his shoot resemble

a 'site' on which each person has his or her place under the architect's direction.

We had to wait to see what this new construction was like. The film was finished early in 2009, and its release was originally planned for September. Meanwhile, in Cannes, Scorsese, as president of his newly set-up World Cinema Foundation, reported on the progress of the organization, which not only restores rare and forgotten films, but also digitizes them and makes them available, sometimes free, on the internet.

Reports and rumours about his projects had proliferated until they formed an impenetrable tangle: Leonardo DiCaprio was supposed to play President Theodore Roosevelt, as well as Frank Sinatra, under his direction. The *Silence* project cropped up regularly in the professional press, with Benicio Del Toro in the lead. Paramount announced a reunion with Robert De Niro, who was to play an Irish-American hitman, working for the Italian mafia in a project to be entitled either *The Irishman* or *I Heard You Paint Houses*. Lastly, the subscription TV channel HBO said Scorsese was to make the pilot and supervise a new series *Boardwalk Empire*, based on a story about the glory days of Atlantic City during Prohibition. Scorsese did in fact direct what was his first episode of a series, in summer 2009.

Just at that moment, Paramount announced that the release of *Shutter Island* was to be postponed until February 2010. The news created a great stir in Hollywood. The studio's motivation was clear; a release in September would have made the film a front-runner at the Oscars, involving a costly campaign on behalf of Scorsese and DiCaprio. In February, the film, whose trailer suggested that it would appeal to thrill-seekers, was released as if it was just another mass-market example of the genre. Like all the big studios, Paramount had been hit by 91

the collapse of its income from DVDs, and was looking for ways of making savings no matter what, even if that meant injuring the dignity of a great director who had only recently won an Oscar.

It was not altogether a surprise to learn, early in 2010, that Scorsese was to make his next film for Warner Bros. It was much more surprising, on the other hand, to learn of its subject matter, taken from an illustrated book for teenagers, Brian Selznick's *The Invention of Hugo Cabret*, published in 2007. This fantasy, set in Paris between the wars, would enable Scorsese to make a film for his daughter (she would be ten years old in 2010), to explore the digital special effects he had been using since he made *Aviator*, while also experimenting with 3-D, and above all, to challenge expectations, even more than he had been ready to do with *Shutter Island*. *Shutter Island*

was presented in Berlin outside competition, and opened in the United States on 19 February 2010. It was an immediate success, and did even better than *The Departed*. In that respect Scorsese could be satisfied, but its critical reception was less unanimous. Todd McCarthy, in *Variety*, compared it to Stanley Kubrick's *The Shining*, but A. O. Scott, in the *New York Times*, thought it was a 'catastrophe'.

The screenplay by Laeta Kalogradis, who had scripted Oliver Stone's *Alexander* (2004), sticks closely to the plot of the novel, which rests on the growing uncertainty of the reader, and now the cinema audience, as to Teddy Daniels's sanity. Suffering from migraines and subject to terrible nightmares, the agent is a hallucinatory version of the heroes of the immediate post-war period who populated the films of Otto Preminger and Fritz Lang. Scorsese himself compares his character with the detective played by Dana Andrews in Preminger's *Laura*, 'a man who is already half out of his mind'.[10]

His mental instability springs from an accumulation of traumas, some private (his wife has died in an arson attack), some historical (Daniels had been a member of the unit that liberated Dachau). These elements are presented explicitly, in dream sequences or flashbacks, and we immediately wonder whether they are memories or reconstructions. Daniels is not Scorsese's first psychopath: before him there was Travis Bickle in *Taxi Driver* and Frank Pierce, the exhausted paramedic played by Nicolas Cage in *Bringing Out the Dead*. Howard Hughes, the aviator, was not himself a model of psychological balance.

Scorsese presents his hero's distorted perceptions with a great skill (and Leonard DiCaprio enters fully into his character's psychotic state). Very early on, the editing and camera angles introduce a sense of growing uncertainty into the story. But the accumulation of cinematic references (Scorsese quotes Jacques Tourneur at length in the interviews that accompanied the film's release), which, heightened by the use of colour and digital effects weighs the film down. It's a (sometimes satisfying) test for any cinephile's powers of assimilation.

Under all this baroque ornamentation, however, we can detect anxieties that are as acute as those that pervade *Mean Streets*. Once again, Scorsese is exploring the furthest limits of human existence. Dennis Lehane's novel encouraged him to venture into territory that he had until then ignored: the Dachau sequences present both Nazi barbarity and the homicidal rage that overcomes the American soldiers when they discover it. Max von Sydow and Ben Kingsley embody, each in his own way (ghostly and enigmatic in Von Sydow's case, voluble and brilliant in Kingsley's), the excesses and abuse of science.

For all that *Shutter Island* is irritating and sometimes disappointing, it leaves a deep impression. At the centre of this horrific labyrinth we find a terrified child, who dramatizes the fears that made him a man, that took possession of him in darkened movie theatres, and rose right up to his windowsill from the streets of Little Italy, teeming with scarcely human down-and-outs and mysterious gangsters.

Opposite page: Martin Scorsese with Leonardo DiCaprio on the set of *Shutter Island* (2010).

Below: Leonardo DiCaprio, Mark Ruffalo and Ben Kingsley in *Shutter Island* (2010).

Chronology

1910
The Scorsese and Cappa families leave Sicily and arrive in New York.

1932
Marriage of Catherine Cappa and Charles Scorsese.

1942
17 November. Martin Scorsese born in Queens.

1946
New York release of *Duel in the Sun*, Scorsese's earliest memory of cinema.

1948
The Scorseses buy a TV set.

1950
The Scorseses leave Queens for Little Italy, and take a small apartment at 253 Elizabeth Street.

1960
Martin Scorsese graduates from high school and enrols at New York University.

1964
18 June. The first short Scorsese makes at NYU, *What's a Nice Girl Like You Doing in a Place Like This?*, wins a prize from the New York Society of Cinematologists. Martin Scorsese shares $10,000 with another winner and graduates Bachelor of Arts, with a major in film, from NYU's Washington Square College.

Martin Scorsese in the 1940s.

Martin Scorsese with his parents in the 1940s.

1965
29 October. *Bring on the Dancing Girls* shown in the auditorium of the Law Faculty of NYU; receives positive review in the *New York Times*.

1967
15 November. *Who's That Knocking at My Door?*, the new title of *Bring on the Dancing Girls*, is presented at the Chicago Film Festival.

1968
Scorsese obtains his master's degree in cinema from NYU and starts teaching there. While in Europe to present *The Big Shave* at the Knokke-le-Zoute festival, he shoots the nude scenes for *Bring on the Dancing Girls*.

1970
Scorsese uses NYU's equipment to coordinate *Street Scenes*, a documentary on the demonstrations against the Vietnam War.

1971
At the beginning of the year, Scorsese moves to Los Angeles, to show the rock documentary *Medicine Ball Caravan*. Roger Corman proposes that he make *Boxcar Bertha*.

1972
14 June. U.S. release of *Boxcar Bertha*.

1973
April to June. Scorsese shoots *Mean Streets* in New York and Los Angeles. **2 October.** The film is presented at the New York Film Festival; opens in cinemas on 14 October.

1974
Shooting of *Alice Doesn't Live Here Anymore*, which opens in Los Angeles on 9 December.

Martin Scorsese with his parents in *Italianamerican* (1974).

1975
8 April. Ellen Burstyn receives the Oscar for best actress for *Alice Doesn't Live Here Anymore*, which is presented in competition at Cannes on 14 May. From June to September, Scorsese shoots *Taxi Driver* in New York.

1976
13 May. *Taxi Driver* is presented at the Cannes Festival. **28 May.** The jury, chaired by Tennessee Williams, awards it the Palme d'Or to criticism in the press. Three days previously, *Mean Streets* had opened in Paris. Scorsese begins shooting *New York, New York*, which is completed in September. During editing, The Band give their last concert, for Thanksgiving, on 3 November, at San Francisco's Winterland. Martin Scorsese films it.

1977
21 June. *New York, New York* opens in the United States. A commercial and critical failure.

1978
26 April. *The Last Waltz* opens. Shooting of *American Boy*, a documentary about his friend Stephen Prince. **September.** Scorsese, sapped by drugs and overwork, is hospitalized. De Niro persuades him to make *Raging Bull*.

1979
Filming of *Raging Bull* begins in April and is interrupted during the summer to allow De Niro to put on thirty kilos. **30 September.** Martin Scorsese marries Isabella Rossellini. At Christmas, he shoots the 'fat scenes', with an almost obese Robert De Niro.

1980
5 April. 'Everything we are doing now means nothing!' – the beginning of a manifesto that Scorsese publishes to warn the public about the loss of cinematic heritage, due to the deterioration of Eastman colour film. **14 November.** New York release of *Raging Bull*.

1981
31 March. Robert De Niro and Thelma Schoonmaker win Oscars, but Scorsese leaves empty-handed. In early June, he begins shooting *The King of Comedy*.

1983
18 February. U.S. release of *The King of Comedy*. **January to September.** Scorsese prepares to shoot *The Last Temptation of Christ*, which Paramount is committed to produce. On Christmas Eve, the studio abandons the project, under pressure from Christian organizations.

1984
Shooting of *After Hours*, in New York.

1985
In Paris, the Minister of Culture, Jack Lang, tries to enable *The Last Temptation of Christ* to benefit from the French funding system. Catholic bishops protest, and the project is abandoned in March. **13 September.** *After Hours* is released in America.

1986
January to April. shooting of *The Color of Money*, which opens on 8 October. **May.** *After Hours* is presented at Cannes, without Scorsese. The jury, chaired by Sidney Pollack, nevertheless awards him the prize for best direction.

Martin Scorsese in 1983.

1987
Autumn. Shooting of *The Last Temptation of Christ* in Morocco. Worldwide publication of the video of Michael Jackson's *Bad*.

1988
11 July. While Scorsese is in New York shooting *Life Lessons*, his contribution to the film *New York Stories*, a coalition of American Christian organizations threatens to boycott the MCA group, of which Universal Studios is a subsidiary, if *The Last Temptation of Christ* is distributed in cinemas. **12 August.** The film opens in the United States before being presented at Venice. **6 September.** French cardinals Lustiger and Decourtray declare, 'We have not seen M. Scorsese's film [...] but we protest in advance against its distribution.'

1989
Shooting of *Goodfellas*.

1990
With support from Woody Allen, Francis Ford Coppola and other filmmakers, Scorsese sets up the Film Foundation, with the aim of preserving the heritage of cinema. **19 September.** American release of *Goodfellas*.

1991
13 November. American release of *Cape Fear*.

1992
March to June. Shooting of *The Age of Innocence*.

1993
23 August. Scorsese's father, Charles, dies at age 80. **31 August.** *The Age of Innocence* is presented at the Venice Film Festival.

Martin Scorsese with Robert De Niro on the set of *Goodfellas* (1990).

1994
Begun in the autumn, shooting of *Casino* is completed in January 1995, in Las Vegas.

1995
3 November. American cinema owners, meeting at ShowEast in Atlantic City, are hostile to *Casino*, which opens in cinemas a few days later. Channel Four distributes it. *A Personal Journey with Martin Scorsese Through American Movies*.

1996
Scorsese returns to Morocco to make *Kundun*.

1997
January. Catherine Scorsese dies at age 84.

1998
13 to 24 May. Scorsese chairs the jury in Cannes. He awards the Palme d'Or to Theo Angelopoulos for *Eternity and a Day*, and the grand jury prize to Roberto Begnini's *Life Is Beautiful*.

1999
At the Venice Festival, Scorsese cancels the presentation of *My Voyage to Italy*, which is finally shown the following year. **22 October.** U.S. premiere of *Bringing Out the Dead*.

2000
18 September. Shooting starts on *Gangs of New York*. It is finished on 12 April the following year.

Martin Scorsese with Leonardo DiCaprio and Cameron Diaz at the 2001 Cannes Film Festival.

2002
9 December. U.S. release of *Gangs of New York*, after problems in post-production, marked by conflicts between Scorsese and the producer, Harvey Weinstein.

2003
23 March. After a campaign by Miramax, the crew of *Gangs of New York* arrives at the Oscars ceremony with ten nominations. They leave without a single statuette. **17 November.** Shooting of *The Aviator*, begun ninety-one days earlier, ends on Scorsese's birthday.

2004
15 July. The series *Martin Scorsese Presents the Blues* is nominated for an Emmy, the American TV award. **14 December.** *The Aviator* opens.

2005
January. TV broadcast of a commercial for American Express in which De Niro, directed by Scorsese, sings the praises of the 'melting-pot' of lower Manhattan and of the credit card simultaneously. **25 April–15 September.** Shooting of *The Departed*. **7 September.** *No Direction Home*, Scorsese's documentary on Bob Dylan, is shown at the Toronto Festival. **11 September.** Paramount announces that it will produce a film on the youth of Theodore Roosevelt, in which Leonardo DiCaprio will again be directed by Scorsese.

2006
6 October. U.S. release of *The Departed* in Boston and New York. With receipts of over $120 million in North America, the film is the biggest commercial success of Scorsese's career. **7 November.** Paramount announces that it has signed a four-year contract under which Scorsese will direct and produce films to be shown in cinemas and on TV, video and the internet. The first item in the contract is the documentary on the Rolling Stones shot in the autumn.

2007
25 February. Scorsese finally wins an Oscar. *The Departed* garners four: for best film, best director, best editing (Thelma Schoonmaker) and best adapted screenplay (William Monahan). In the summer, *The Key to Reserva*, a commercial for sparkling wine in the form of a Hitchcock pastiche, is shown in Spanish cinemas.

2008
8 March. Shooting starts on *Shutter Island*. **October.** Paramount announces that it will fund *I Heard You Paint Houses*, the story of an Irish hitman working for the mafia, with De Niro in the lead.

2009
At the Cannes Film Festival, Scorsese presents the digital version of the World Cinema Foundation and lets slip the information that he is to direct a biography of Frank Sinatra. **21 August.** Paramount announces that the release of *Shutter Island*, set for 2 October, has been postponed to 19 February 2010, taking it out of the running for the Oscars. **1 September.** HBO announces that it is giving the go-ahead to the series *Boardwalk Empire*, which Scorsese is to produce and for which he will make the pilot.

2010
13 February. A week before its American release, *Shutter Island* is shown outside competition at the 60th Berlin Film Festival. On the way there, Scorsese stops in Paris to look for locations for *The Invention of Hugo Cabret*, which he is due to shoot in the summer. *Shutter Island* opens in the United States on 18 February, and breaks all records for Scorsese, taking $40 million over its first weekend.

Martin Scorsese with The Rolling Stones in 2006.

Filmography

PRODUCER ONLY

Medicine Ball   1971
Caravan
by François Reichenbach

The Grifters   1990
by Stephen Frears

Naked in New York   1993
by Daniel Algrant

Mad Dog and Glory   1993
by John McNaughton

Con gli occhi chiusi   1994
by Francesca Archibugi

Search and Destroy   1995
by David Salle

Clockers   1995
by Spike Lee

Grace of My Heart   1996
by Allison Anders

Kicked in the Head   1997
by Matthew Harrison

The Hi-Lo Country   1998
by Stephen Frears

You Can Count on Me 2000
by Kenneth Lonergan

Rain   2001
by Katherine Lindberg

Deuces Wild   2002
by Scott Kalvert

The Soul of a Man   2003
by Wim Wenders

Lightning in a Bottle   2004
by Antoine Fuqua

Brides (Nyfes)   2004
by Pantelis Voulgaris

Picasso and Braque   2008
Go to the Movies
by Arne Glimcher

Lymelife   2008
by Derick Martini

The Young Victoria   2009
by Jean-Marc Vallée

ACTOR ONLY

Cannonball!   1976
by Paul Bartel

Il pap'occhio   1980
by Renzo Arbore

Anna Pavlova   1983
by Emil Loteanu

'Round Midnight   1986
by Bertrand Tavernier

Dreams   1990
by Akira Kurosawa

Guilty by Suspicion   1991
by Irwin Winkler

Quiz Show   1994
by Robert Redford

Search and Destroy   1995
by David Salle

Shark Tale   2004
by Bibo Bergeron,
Vicky Jenson and Rob Letterman

SHORT FILMS

What's a Nice Girl   1963
Like You Doing
in a Place Like This?
B&W. **Format** 16mm. **Running time** 9 mins. With Zeph Michaelis, Mimi Stark, Martin Scorsese.
• A young man, obsessed by a painting, tries in vain to find help in marriage and psychoanalysis.

It's Not Just You,   1964
Murray!
B&W. **Format** 16mm. **Running time** 15 mins. With Ira Rubin, Sam De Fazio, Andrea Martin, Catherine Scorsese.
• Forty years in the life of two Italian-Americans, from Prohibition to the 1960s.

The Big Shave   1967
Format 16mm. **Running time** 6 mins. With Peter Bernuth.
• In his bathroom, a man takes his daily shaving routine to the point of self-mutilation.

Italianamerican   1974
Format 16mm. **Running time** 48 mins. With Charles, Catherine and Martin Scorsese.
• Over a weekend, Martin Scorsese talks to his parents about their history and their community: his grandparents, who emigrated from Sicily around 1900, the neighbourhood of Little Italy and a culture dominated by mealtime rituals.

American Boy: 1978
A Profile of Steven Prince
Format 16mm. **Running time** 55 mins.
• Scorsese recounts the tumultuous, hilarious, criminal career of his friend and collaborator Steven Prince.

Bad   1987
Format video. **Running time** 16 mins. With Michael Jackson, Wesley Snipes, Roberta Flack, Charles and Catherine Scorsese.
• Video made to accompany the second single extracted from the album of the same name. The song is accompanied by a prelude contrasting the 'nice' Daryl with the 'bad' Mini Max, played by Wesley Snipes, then starting his career.

Life Lessons   1989
Format 16mm. **Running time** 44 mins. With Nick Nolte, Patrick O'Neal, Rosanna Arquette, Steve Buscemi.
• From a message on his answering machine, a successful New York painter learns that his girlfriend is about to leave her. With Francis Ford Coppola's Life without Zoe and Woody Allen's Oedipus Wrecks, Life Lessons makes up the trilogy New York Stories.

Made in Milan   1990
B&W. **Format** 35mm. **Running time** 27 mins. With Giorgio Armani.
• The founder of the ready-to-wear label describes his city and his life and presents his new collection.

TELEVISION FILMS

Mirror, Mirror   1985
Running time 24 mins. With Sam Waterston, Helen Shaver.
• A writer of horror stories is persecuted by a ghost. Made at Steven Spielberg's request, for the TV series Amazing Stories.

A Personal Journey   1995
with Martin Scorsese
Through American Movies
Running time 3h 45. Co-directed by Michael Henry Wilson.
• A three-part history of the first hundred years of American cinema, and the autobiography of a child with a passion for the art that he made his own.

My Voyage to Italy   1999
Il Mio Viaggio In Italia
Running time 4h 06.
• In the form of an ensemble of long extracts, this is an invitation to discover Italian cinema. The journey concentrates on the years between the birth of neo-realism, at the end of World War II, and the invention of modernity by Antonioni.

The Neighborhood   2001
Running time 7 mins.
• Shot just after the attacks of 11 September 2001, the film shows Scorsese visiting what remains of Little Italy. With his daughter, Francesca, he meets the last survivors of his parents' generation.

'Feel Like Going   2003
Home: The Blues From
Africa to the New World'
Running time 1h 23. With John Lee Hooker, Salif Keita, Taj Mahal, Ali Farka Touré.
• The first episode of a TV series on the blues produced by Scorsese, the film follows the musician Corey Harris, who goes to Mali in search of the roots of the blues. His quest then takes him to Mississippi, the cradle of blues music.

Lady by the Sea,   2003
The Statue of Liberty
Running time 46 mins. Co-directed by Kent Jones.
• A TV documentary made on the eve of the reopening of the Statue of Liberty, closed since 11 September 2001. A reflection on the symbol of the Constitution of the American nation.

No Direction Home: 2005
Bob Dylan
Running time 3h 27. With Bob Dylan, Joan Baez, Allen Ginsberg.
• A montage of archival material and recent interviews, tracing Bob Dylan's personal and artistic life from 1941 to 1966.

Boardwalk Empire   2010
With Jessica Caiola, Steve Buscemi, Michael Stuhlbarg, Kelly Mcdonald.
• The pilot for a TV series commissioned by the subscription channel Home Box Office (HBO). The action starts on 16 January 1920, the date on which Prohibition came into force, in Atlantic City, the Babylon of the eastern United States.

COMMERCIALS

Advertisement   1986
for Armani (I)
B&W. **Running time** 30 sec.

Advertisement   1988
for Armani (II)
Running time 20 sec.

Advertisement for   2005
American Express
Cinematography   Robert Richardson. **Running time** 1 min. 30 sec. With Robert De Niro, Martin Scorsese.

The Key to Reserva   2007
Running time 10 mins. With Simon Baker, Kelli O'Hara, Michael Stuhlbarg.
• This long advertisement for cava, the Catalan sparkling wine, was shown in Spanish cinemas in summer 2007. In it, we see Scorsese pretending to have found a page from a lost screenplay by Alfred Hitchcock. This sequence follows a mixture of key moments from Notorious and The Man Who Knew Too Much. It is a pastiche made with fanatical care.

FEATURE FILMS

Who's That Knocking 1969 at My Door?

B&W. **Screenplay** Martin Scorsese. **Cinematography** Michael Wadleigh, Richard H. Coll and Max Fisher. **Editing** Thelma Schoonmaker. **Production** Joseph Weill, Betzi and Haig Manoogian. **Music** Mitch Ryder and the Detroit Wheels, The Doors, The Bellnotes, The Chantells and others. **Production** Tri-Mod, presented by Joseph Brenner Associates. **Running time** 1h 35. With Harvey Keitel (J.R.), Zina Bethune (the young girl), Anne Colette (the young girl in the dream).

• An alter ego of Martin Scorsese, J.R. is a very young man from Little Italy, torn between the spirit and the flesh, ambition and the desire to stay within his community. He drifts around New York with his friends and experiences his first sexual excitements.

Street Scenes 1970

Production Martin Scorsese, New York Cinetracts Collective. **Running time** 1h 15.

• A collective documentary about the demonstrations against the Vietnam War in New York and on Wall Street, of which Scorsese directed the last sequence.

Boxcar Bertha 1972

Screenplay Joyce Hooper and John William Carrington, based on Ben L. Reitman's *Sister of the Road*. **Cinematography** John Stephens. **Editing** Buzz Feitshans. **Music** Gib Guilbeau, Thad Maxwell. **Production** Roger Corman. **Running time** 1h 28. With Barbara Hershey (Bertha Thompson), David Carradine (Big Bill Shelly), Barry Primus (Rake Brown), Bernie Casey (Von Morton), John Carradine (H. Buckram Sartoris).

• The amorous flight of orphan

Bertha and the anarchist trade unionist Big Bill Shelly, in Arkansas during the Depression.

Mean Streets 1973

Screenplay Martin Scorsese, Mardik Martin. **Cinematography** Kent Wakeford. **Editing** Sid Levin, Martin Scorsese. **Music** The Rolling Stones, The Chantells, The Marvelettes and others. **Production** Jonathan T. Taplin. **Running time** 1h 50. With Robert De Niro (Johnny Boy), Harvey Keitel (Charlie), David Proval (Tony), Amy Robinson (Teresa), Richard Romanus (Michael).

• On the streets of Little Italy, between the church and the cafés frequented by members of the Mafia, Charlie tries to become a man. In his wake, Johnny Boy, terrifying and stuck in adolescence, wreaks havoc.

Alice Doesn't Live Here Anymore 1974

Screenplay Robert Getchell. **Cinematography** Kent Wakeford. **Editing** Marcia Lucas. **Music** Richard LaSalle. **Production** David Susskind, Audrey Maas, Larry Cohen. **Running time** 1h 52. With Ellen Burstyn (Alice Hyatt), Kris Kristofferson (David), Alfred Lutter (Tommy), Diane Ladd (Flo), Jodie Foster (Audrey), Harvey Keitel (Ben).

• After her husband's death, Alice leaves New Mexico with her twelve-year-old son. She wants to get to California to resume her singing career. On the road, she stops in Arizona where she takes a job as a waitress.

Taxi Driver 1976

Screenplay Paul Schrader. **Cinematography** Michael Chapman. **Art direction** Charles Rosen. **Production design** Herbert Mulligan. **Editing** Marcia Lucas, Tom Rolf, Melvin Shapiro. **Music** Bernard Herrmann. **Production** Julia Phillips, Michael Phillips, Phillip M. Goldfarb. **Running time** 1h 53.

With Robert De Niro (Travis Bickle), Cybill Shepherd (Betsy), Peter Boyle (Wizard), Albert Brooks (Tom), Leonard Harris (Charles Palantine), Harvey Keitel (Sport/Matthew), Jodie Foster (Iris), Martin Scorsese (the passenger with the Magnum 44).

• Haunted by his memories of Vietnam, Travis Bickle, an ex-Marine, gets a job as a taxi driver in New York. He thinks he is in love with a young blonde woman, an aide to a candidate in the presidential election. After he is rejected, he decides to rescue a teenage prostitute, and punish the people who have led her astray.

New York, New York 1977

Screenplay Earl Mac Rauch, Mardik Martin. **Cinematography** Laszlo Kovacs. **Production design** Boris Leven. **Editing** Irving Lerner, Marcia Lucas, Tom Rolf, Bertram Lovitt. **Music supervision** Ralph Burns. **Original songs** John Kander and Fred Ebb. **Production** Robert Chartoff, Irwin Winkler. **Running time** As released 2h 16, complete version 2h 43. With Liza Minnelli (Francine Evans), Robert De Niro (Jimmy Doyle), Lionel Stander (Tony Harwell), Barry Primus (Paul Wilson), Mary Kay Place (Bernice), Georgie Auld (Frankie Harte), Clarence Clemons (Cecil Powell).

• Spanning 1945 to 1955, and the tumultuous love life of Jimmy Doyle, a temperamental saxophonist, not gifted enough to be a star, and Francine Evans, a talented singer who turns her back on jazz to make a career in Hollywood.

The Last Waltz 1978

Cinematography Michael Chapman, Laszlo Kovacs, Vilmos Zsigmond, David Myers, Bobby Byrne, Michael Watkins, Hiro Narita. **Production design** Boris Leven. **Editing** Yeu-Bun Yee, Jan Roblee. **Music** The Band and guests. **Production** Robbie Robertson and Jonathan Taplin. **Running time** 1h 57.

• The last concert by The Band, performing at Winterland, San Francisco, on Thanksgiving 1976. Guest per-

formers include Bob Dylan and Eric Clapton. Scorsese added interviews and songs filmed in the studio to the scenes of the live performance.

Raging Bull 1980

B&W. **Screenplay** Paul Schrader, Mardik Martin, based on *Raging Bull* by Jake LaMotta, Joseph Carter and Peter Savage (1970). **Cinematography** Michael Chapman. **Production design** Gene Rudolf. **Editing** Thelma Schoonmaker. **Sound** Frank Warner. **Music** Aaron Copland, Mascagni, Ella Fitzgerald and others. **Production** Irwin Winkler, Robert Chartoff. **Running time** 2h 08. With Robert De Niro (Jake LaMotta), Cathy Moriarty (Vickie LaMotta), Joe Pesci (Joey LaMotta), Frank Vincent (Salvy), Johnny Barnes (Sugar Ray Robinson), Louis Raftis (Marcel Cerdan).

• The decline of Jake LaMotta, champion boxer and a corrupt and violent man, who reached the lowest depths in prison before turning to show business.

The King of Comedy 1983

Screenplay Paul D. Zimmerman. **Cinematography** Fred Schuler. **Production design** Boris Leven. **Editing** Thelma Schoonmaker. **Music** Robbie Robertson. **Production** Arnon Milchan, Robert Greenhut. **Running time** 1h 49. With Robert De Niro (Rupert Pupkin), Jerry Lewis (Jerry Langford), Diahnne Abbott (Rita), Sandra Bernhard (Masha).

• Rupert Pupkin wants to be as famous as his idol, Jerry Langford, a fictional version of Johnny Carson, the presenter of *The Tonight Show* on NBC. When Langford will not invite him to appear on the show, Pupkin plots to kidnap him.

After Hours 1985

Screenplay Joseph Minion. **Cinematography** Michael Ballhaus. **Editing** Thelma Schoonmaker. **Music** Howard Shore. **Production**

Amy Robinson, Griffin Dunne, Robert F. Colesberry. **Running time** 1h 37. With Griffin Dunne (Paul Hackett), Rosanna Arquette (Marcy), Verna Bloom (June), Linda Fiorentino (Kiki), Teri Garr (Julie), John Heard (Tom, the barman).

• In lower Manhattan, in the still bohemian neighbourhood of SoHo, Paul Hackett, a computer programmer, whose judgement is disturbed when he meets the irresistible Marcy, sees his evening of pleasure turn into a nightmare.

The Color of Money 1986
Screenplay Richard Price, based on the novel by Walter Tevis. **Cinematography** Michael Ballhaus. **Production design** Boris Leven. **Editing** Thelma Schoonmaker. **Music** Robbie Robertson. **Production** Irving Axelrad, Barbara De Fina. **Running time** 1h 59. With Paul Newman ('Fast Eddie' Felson), Tom Cruise (Vincent Lauria), Mary Elizabeth Mastrantonio (Carmen), Helen Shaver (Janelle), John Turturro (Julian), Forest Whitaker (Amos).

• Twenty-five years after the ending of *The Hustler* (Robert Rossen, 1961), 'Fast Eddie' Nelson returns to the world of pool and takes under his wing a young prodigy, Vincent Lauria. Eddie gradually regains the desire to play, and confronts his protégé at a championship.

The Last 1988
Temptation of Christ
Screenplay Paul Schrader (and Jay Cocks, not credited), based on the novel by Nikos Kazantzakis. **Cinematography** Michael Ballhaus. **Production design** John Beard. **Editing** Thelma Schoonmaker. **Music** Peter Gabriel. **Production** Barbara De Fina. Harry Ufland, Frank Dileo. **Running time** 2h 43. With Willem Dafoe (Jesus), Harvey Keitel (Judas), Verna Bloom (Mary, mother of Jesus), Barbara Hershey (Mary Magdalene), John Lurie (The Apostle James), Andre Gregory (John the Baptist), Harry Dean Stanton (Saul/Paul), David Bowie (Pontius Pilate), Juliette Caton (The angel).

• As a carpenter in Nazareth, Jesus supplies the Romans with crosses, resisting both Judas's calls to political revolt and the voice of God. When he does submit to God, the temptation to be human pursues him all the way to the cross.

Goodfellas 1990
Screenplay Nicholas Pileggi, Martin Scorsese, based on Nicholas Pileggi's *Wiseguy*. **Cinematography** Michael Ballhaus. **Production design** Kristi Zea. **Editing** Thelma Schoonmaker. **Credit titles** Saul and Elaine Bass. **Music** The Rolling Stones, The Moonglows, The Cleftones, Giuseppe Di Stefano and others. **Production** Irwin Winkler, Barbara De Fina. **Running time** 2h 26. With Robert De Niro (James Conway), Ray Liotta (Henry Hill), Joe Pesci (Tommy De Vito), Lorraine Bracco (Karen Hill), Paul Sorvino (Paul Cicero), Frank Sivero (Frankie Carbone).

• Half Italian and half Irish, Henry Hill wants to be a full member of the mob, but is prevented by his mixed background. But he still tries to win a place by imitating his mentors. His addiction to cocaine forces him to betray his associates.

Cape Fear 1991
Screenplay Wesley Strick, based on the 1962 screenplay by James R. Webb and the novel by John D. MacDonald. **Cinematography** Freddie Francis. **Editing** Thelma Schoonmaker. **Music** Bernard Herrmann, adapted by Elmer Bernstein. **Production** Barbara De Fina, Kathleen Kennedy, Frank Marchhall. **Running time** 2h 08. With Robert De Niro (Max Cady), Nick Nolte (Sam Bowden), Jessica Lange (Leigh Bowden), Juliette Lewis (Danielle Bowden), Robert Mitchum (Lieutenant Elgart), Gregory Peck (Lee Heller), Martin Balsam (the judge).

• Max Cady, a criminal psychopath recently released from prison, wants to take revenge on his lawyer, Sam Bowden, and starts to terrorize Bowden and his family. A remake of the film by Jack Lee Thompson (1962).

The Age of Innocence 1993
Screenplay Jay Cocks, Martin Scorsese, based on the novel by Edith Wharton (1920). **Cinematography** Michael Ballhaus. **Production design** Dante Ferretti. **Costumes** Gabriella Pescucci. **Editing** Thelma Schoonmaker. **Credit titles** Elaine and Saul Bass. **Music** Elmer Bernstein. **Production** Barbara De Fina. **Running time** 2h 18. With Daniel Day-Lewis (Newland Archer), Michelle Pfeiffer (Ellen Olenska), Winona Ryder (May Welland), Miriam Margolyes (Mrs Manson Mingott), Richard E. Grant (Larry Lefferts).

• In New York, around 1870, Newland Archer, an affluent lawyer, is about to marry an heiress, May Welland. The return to the city of his cousin, Ellen Olenska, unhappily married to a European aristocrat, threatens to bring down the edifice of social convention.

Casino 1995
Screenplay Nicholas Pileggi, Martin Scorsese, based on Nicholas Pileggi's *Casino* (1995). **Cinematography** Robert Richardson. **Production design** Dante Ferretti. **Editing** Thelma Schoonmaker. **Credit titles** Elaine and Saul Bass. **Music** Bach, The Rolling Stones, Louis Prima, Dean Martin, Roxy Music and others. **Production** Barbara De Fina. **Running time** 2h 57. With Robert De Niro (Sam 'Ace' Rothstein), Sharon Stone (Ginger McKenna), Joe Pesci (Nicky Santoro), James Woods (Lester Diamond), Don Rickles (Billy Sherbert), Alan King (Andy Stone), Kevin Pollack (Phillip Green).

• The rise and fall of 'Ace' Rothstein, sent to Las Vegas in 1972 by the Chicago Italian Mafia. He impresses with his efficiency until he marries Ginger, a prostitute and cocaine addict.

Kundun 1997
Screenplay and co-production Melissa Mathison. **Cinematography**

Roger Deakins. **Production design and costumes** Dante Ferretti. **Editing** Thelma Schoonmaker. **Music** Philip Glass. **Production** Barbara De Fina. **Running time** 2h 14. With Tenzin Thuthob Tsarong (the adult Dalai Lama), Gyurme Tethong (the twelve-year-old Dalai Lama), Tencho Gyalpo (the mother), Tenzin Topjar (Lobsang aged from five to ten), Tsewang Migyur Khangsar (the father), Tenzin Lodoe (Takster).

• The life of the fourteenth Dalai Lama, from the time he was recognized at the age of five, to the Chinese invasion of Tibet in 1959.

Bringing Out 1999
the Dead
Screenplay Paul Schrader, based on Joe Connelly's *Bringing Out the Dead* (1998). **Cinematography** Robert Richardson. **Production design** Dante Ferretti. **Editing** Thelma Schoonmaker. **Music** Elmer Bernstein, with songs by Van Morrison, Johnny Thunders, the Clash & others. **Production** Barbara De Fina, Scott Rudin. **Running time** 2h 01. With Nicolas Cage (Frank Pierce), Patricia Arquette (Mary Burke), John Goodman (Larry), Ving Rhames (Marcus), Tom Sizemore (Tom Walls), Marc Anthony (Noel).

• Every night, Frank Pierce crisscrosses Manhattan in his ambulance, transporting the injured and the dying. Numbed by lack of sleep, he staggers between hallucinations and an aspiration to redemption, between the recurrent image of a young woman he was unable to save and Mary, the daughter of a heart attack victim.

Gangs of New York 2002
Screenplay Jay Cocks, Steven Zaillian, Kenneth Lonergan, based on *The Gangs of New York* by Herbert Asbury (1928). **Cinematography** Michael Ballhaus. **Production design** Dante Ferretti. **Costumes** Sandy Powell. **Editing** Thelma Schoonmaker. **Music** Howard Shore. **Production** Alberto Grimaldi, Harvey Weinstein, Michael Ovitz, Graham King. **Running time** 2h 48.

With Leonardo DiCaprio (Amsterdam Vallon), Daniel Day-Lewis (Bill 'The Butcher' Cutting), Cameron Diaz (Jenny Everdeane), Jim Broadbent (William 'Boss' Tweed), John C. Reilly (Happy Jack), Henry Thomas (Johnny Sirocco), Liam Neeson ('Priest' Vallon).

• Fifteen years after the murder of his father by Bill Cutting, Amsterdam Vallon returns to the Five Points bent on revenge. In this slum neighbourhood of lower Manhattan, in the middle of the Civil War, the United States was being constructed, among communal conflicts and the birth of organized crime.

The Aviator   2004
Screenplay John Logan. **Cinematography** Robert Richardson. **Production design** Dante Feretti. **Editing** Thelma Schoonmaker. **Music** Howard Shore and popular songs of the day. **Production** Michael Mann, Sandy Climan, Graham King, Charles Evans, Jr. **Running time** 2h 49. With Leonardo DiCaprio (Howard Hughes), Cate Blanchett (Katharine Hepburn), Kate Beckinsale (Ava Gardner), John C. Reilly (Noah Dietrich), Alec Baldwin (Juan Trippe), Alan Alda (Senator Ralph Owen Brewster), Ian Holm (Professor Fitz), Danny Huston (Jack Frye), Gwen Stefani (Jean Harlow), Jude Law (Errol Flynn).

• The irresistible rise of Howard Hughes, a Texas multi-millionaire, in Hollywood and in the air. An independent film producer, brilliant aviator and ruthless businessman, Hughes is shown from his birth in 1927 until his retirement, caused by the increasing severity of his phobias.

The Departed   2006
Screenplay William Monahan, based on the screenplay of *Infernal Affairs* by Siu Fai-mak and Felix Chong (2002). **Cinematography** Michael Ballhaus. **Production design** Kristi Zea. **Editing** Thelma Schoonmaker. **Music** Howard Shore, The Rolling Stones, Van Morrison, John Lennon and others. **Production** Martin Scorsese, Graham King,

Brad Pitt. **Running time** 2h 31. With Leonardo DiCaprio (Billy Costigan), Matt Damon (Colin Sullivan), Jack Nicholson (Frank Costello), Vera Farmiga (Madolyn), Mark Wahlberg (Dignam), Alec Baldwin (Ellerby), Martin Sheen (Captain Queenan).

• Billy Costigan is sent by the Boston police to infiltrate the Irish mob, led by Frank Costello, a bloodthirsty monster. Meanwhile, Costello instructs Colin Sullivan to join the police, to supply him with information. The destinies of these two young men collide in an explosion of violence.

Shine a Light   2008
Cinematography Robert Richardson. **Editing** David Tedeschi. **Music** The Rolling Stones. **Production** Steve Bing, Michael Cohl. **Running time** 2h 02. With The Rolling Stones.

• On two evenings in 2006, The Rolling Stones gave up their rock venue for New York's attractive Beacon Theatre. In the auditorium and on stage, we see various prestigious guests, including Bill and Hillary Clinton, Jack White and Christina Aguilera. Scorsese went to enormous lengths to capture Mick Jagger's every grimace and gesticulation, Keith Richards's smallest false note. Intercut with archive material and comic interludes, *Shine a Light* is a film about the passage of time.

Shutter Island   2010
Screenplay Laeta Kalogridis, based on a novel by Dennis Lehane. **Cinematography** Robert Richardson. **Production design** Dante Ferreti. **Editing** Thelma Schoonmaker. **Music** Robbie Robertson. **Production** Mike Medavoy, Arnold Messer, Brad Fischer. **Running time** 2h 18. With Leonardo DiCaprio (Teddy Daniels), Mark Ruffalo (Chuck Aule), Ben Kingsley (Dr. John Cawley), Michelle Williams (Dolores Chanal), Max von Sydow (Dr. Jeremiah Naehring).

• In 1954, federal marshals Teddy Daniels and Chuck Aule cross Boston Bay on their way to the Shutter Island psychiatric hospital, where the most dangerous psycho-

paths are held. Their job is to investigate the disappearance of a patient who had killed her child, and they meet with hostility from the medical staff, led by Dr Cawley. Teddy Daniels is haunted by memories of his wife, who died in a fire, and by images of the liberation of Dachau, in which he took part. Their investigation comes to a standstill, and a storm cuts the island off from the rest of the world.

Selected Bibliography

Peter Biskind,
Easy Riders, Raging Bulls,
Simon & Schuster, New York, 1998.

Ian Christie and David Thompson,
Scorsese on Scorsese,
Faber and Faber, London, 2004.

Roger Ebert and Martin Scorsese,
Ebert on Scorsese,
University of Chicago Press, Chicago,
2008.

Mary Pat Kelly,
Martin Scorsese: The First Decade,
Redgrave Publishing, Pleasantville,
New York, 1980.

Thomas R. Lindlof,
*Hollywood under Siege:
Martin Scorsese, the Religious Right,
and the Culture Wars*,
University Press of Kentucky,
Lexington, 2008.

Martin Scorsese and
Michael Henry Wilson,
*A Personal Journey Through
American Movies*,
Faber and Faber, London, 1998.

Notes

1. *Martin Scorsese: entretiens avec Michael Henry Wilson*, Cahiers du cinema/Centre Georges-Pompidou, Paris, 2005.

2. *New York Times*, 1 November 1965.

3. Ian Christie and David Thompson, *Scorsese on Scorsese*, Faber and Faber, London, 2004, p.34.

4. Peter Biskind, *Easy Riders, Raging Bulls*, Simon & Schuster, New York, 1998, p.239.

5. Ian Christie and David Thompson, *Scorsese on Scorsese*, Faber and Faber, London, 2004, p.63.

6. As he tells it in the bonus material on the DVD of the film.

7. Ian Christie and David Thompson, *Scorsese on Scorsese*, Faber and Faber, London, 2004, p.76–7.

8. Peter Biskind, *Easy Riders, Raging Bulls*, Simon & Schuster, New York, 1998.

9. In Martin Scorsese's *My Voyage to Italy*.

10. Thomas Sotinel, 'J'ai eté affecté par la peur dans la salle de cinéma' ['I felt frightened at the movies'] (interview with Martin Scorsese), *Le Monde*, 24 February 2010.

Sources

Collection Cahiers du cinéma: inside front cover, pp.2, 4–5, 14, 16, 18, 20, 24, 25, 26 (bottom), 27 (bottom), 36–7, 40–1, 46, 47, 51, 55, 58, 61, 62–3, 64, 65, 66–7, 70, 72 (top), 73, 74 (left), 78, 83 (bottom), 84–5, 86, 92–3, 94, 95, 96 (4th col.), 97 (4th col.), 99 (1st col. top; 2nd col. top and bottom; 4th col. top and bottom), 100 (3rd col.), 101 (1st col. bottom; 2nd col. bottom), inside back cover.
Collection CAT'S: pp.43, 68–9, 88, 90, 91, 101 (2nd col. top).

Martin Scorsese collection: pp.6, 7, 8–9, 10, 11 (bottom), 12, 13, 17, 22–3, 26–7, 29 (top), 33, 34, 35, 36 (bottom), 38, 39, 42, 44, 45, 48–9, 50, 52–3, 54, 56–7, 59, 60, 72 (bottom), 74 (right), 75, 76, 77, 80, 81, 82–3, 87, 96 (1st and 2nd col.), 99 (1st col. middle; 2nd col. middle; 3rd col.; 4th col. middle), 100 (1st, 2nd and 4th col.), 101 (1st col. top).
Michael Henry Wilson Collection: pp.19, 28, 29 (bottom), 99 (1st col. bottom).
Screen grabs: pp.11 (top), 32.
The Kobal Collection: pp.30–1.

Credits

© Courtesy of 20th Century Fox: pp.44, 45, 50, 99 (4th col. middle).
© Camera 5/Ken Rigan: p.36 (bottom).
© Courtesy of Columbia Pictures: pp.8–9, 28, 29, 30–1, 32, 33, 61, 62–3, 99 (2nd col. bottom), 100 (3rd col. top), inside back cover.
© Courtesy of De Fina-Cappa/Paramount Pictures: pp.72 (bottom), 73, 100 (4th col. top).
© Courtesy of Disney/Touchstone/Miramax: pp.48–9, 51, 59, 70, 75, 76, 77, 78, 100 (1st col. top; 3rd col. bottom; 4th col. bottom).

© Nicolas Guérin: cover.
© INA/Norbert Perreau: p.64 (bottom).
© Courtesy of Initial Entertainment Group/Miramax/Warner Bros: pp.74 (right), 80, 81, 82–3, 101 (1st col. top).
© Maureen Lambray: p.96 (4th col. top).
© Lux Films: p.64 (top).
© Courtesy of MGM: pp.2, 14, 19, 27 (bottom), 34, 35, 36–7, 38, 40–1, 42, 43, 74 (left), 99 (1st col. bottom; 3rd col.; 4th col.).
© Motion Picture & Radio Presentations/New York University Department of Television/Summer Motion Picture Workshop:

p.11 (bottom).
© New Empire Films/Scorsese Films: p.39.
© New York Cinetracts Collective: p.11 (top).
© New York University: pp.12, 13.
© Paramount Classics: pp.92–3, 94, 95, 97 (4th col.), 101 (2nd col.).
© Paramount Classics/Jacob Cohl: p.90.
© Paramount Classics/Kevin Mazur: pp.88, 91.
© Paramount/Touchstone Pictures: pp.4–5.
© Martin Scorsese: pp.10, 96 (1st and 2nd col.).
© Traverso: pp.72 (top), 97 (3th col.).

© Trimod Films: pp.16, 99 (1st col. top).
© Courtesy of Universal Pictures: inside front cover, pp.46, 52–3, 54, 60, 66–7, 68–9, 100 (1st col. bottom; 2nd col. bottom; 3rd col. middle).
© Courtesy of Warner Bros Entertainment: pp.18, 20, 22–3, 24, 25, 26 (bottom), 26–7, 47, 55, 56–7, 58, 83 (bottom), 86, 96 (4th col. bottom), 99 (2nd col. top and middle; 4th col. bottom), 100 (2nd col. top), 101 (1st col. bottom).
© Courtesy of Warner Bros Entertainment/Andrew Cooper: pp.84–5, 87.
© Pierre-René Worms: p.65.

All reasonable efforts have been made to trace the copyright holders of the photographs used in this book. We apologize to anyone that we were unable to reach.

Cover: Martin Scorsese photographed by Nicolas Guérin in 2007.
Inside front cover: Robert De Niro and Sharon Stone in *Casino* (1995).
Inside back cover: Robert De Niro in *Taxi Driver* (1976).

Cahiers du cinéma Sarl
65, rue Montmartre
75002 Paris

www.cahiersducinema.com

Revised English edition © 2010 Cahiers du cinéma Sarl
First published in French as *Martin Scorsese* © 2007 Cahiers du cinéma Sarl

ISBN 978 2 8664 2574 6

A CIP catalogue record of this book is available from the British Library.

Series conceived by Claudine Paquot
Designed by Werner Jeker/Les Ateliers du Nord
Translated by Imogen Forster
Printed in China